THE FAMILY DINNER COOKBOOK

Recipes and Inspiration for Quality Time Together

BARBOUR
PUBLISHING

D1042807

Published by Barbour Publishing, Inc., P.O. Box 719, Uhrichsville, Ohio 44683, www.barbourbooks.com

Our mission is to publish and distribute inspirational products offering exceptional value and biblical encouragement to the masses.

Member of the
Evangelical Christian
Publishers Association

Printed in the United States of America.

CONTENTS

INTRODUCTION

Give us this day our daily bread.
And forgive us our debts,
as we forgive our debtors.
And lead us not into temptation,
but deliver us from evil:
For thine is the kingdom, and the power,
and the glory, for ever. Amen.

MATTHEW 6:11–13 KJV

Featuring blessings and prayers, plus memorable scripture selections and inspirational quotes, this delightful cookbook was created with families in mind.

My prayer is that your family would come together to share meals, bond with one another, and truly celebrate the presence and light of Christ in your home.

Each day is a gift!

In Christ Alone,
MariLee Parrish

KID-FRIENDLY FAVORITES

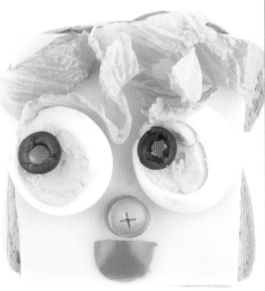

*"I came that they may have life
and have it abundantly."*

JOHN 10:10 ESV

HAM AND CHEESE BREAKFAST SANDWICH

8 eggs
¼ cup milk
Butter
1 small sweet onion, chopped
6 slices deli ham

Salt and pepper to taste
6 slices American cheese
8 slices white bread, toasted
  and buttered
1 medium tomato, sliced thin

Scramble eggs with milk in buttered skillet. Add onion, ham, salt, and pepper. Cook for 5 to 6 minutes. Add cheese. Allow eggs to sit until cheese is melted. Scoop onto buttered toast and add tomato; top with toast. Makes 4 sandwiches.

STRAWBERRY CREAM CHEESE CREPES

⅔ cup milk
2 eggs
2 tablespoons sugar
6 tablespoons flour

2 tablespoons butter
Strawberry preserves
Cream cheese

In blender, mix first four ingredients. Heat butter in small frying pan. Pour one-quarter of batter into pan. Flip when edges are brown. Recipe makes 4 crepes. Fill each crepe with 1 teaspoon preserves and 2 teaspoons cream cheese. Roll and serve.

START THE DAY RIGHT

Breakfast can be a delightful opportunity to set the tone of your family's entire day. Rise before the rest of the crew wakes up and get things started. If you're not a morning person, ask the Lord to give you His supernatural strength to greet each of your family members with a smile and help them start their morning. Prepare a healthy breakfast and pray together as a family. Pray a blessing over each child, such as the following:

Heavenly Father,

I thank You for my son, Jake. Go before him as he heads to school and prepare his heart for whatever comes his way today. Remind him of Your love and constant presence all day long. Help him to remember that he is a precious child of God who is able to do absolutely anything through the power of Christ. Shine Your light in Him so that everyone he meets today will know that he loves You. Amen.

OMELET IN A MUG

2 eggs
2 tablespoons milk
Dash salt

Dash pepper
2 tablespoons shredded
    cheddar cheese

In small bowl, combine eggs, milk, salt, and pepper. Beat well.
Pour into 16-ounce microwavable mug or other dish. Microwave
on high 1 minute. Stir and top with cheese. Microwave for an
additional 30 seconds or until eggs are firm. Stir and serve.

GRILLED BACON AND CHEESE

Butter
4 slices wheat bread

2 slices cheddar cheese
4 slices bacon, cooked

Spread butter on one side of each slice of bread. Fill each
sandwich with cheese and bacon. Cook in skillet for 2 minutes
on first side; then flip and cook another 2 minutes or until
golden brown.

MEXICAN EGGS

2 tablespoons butter
½ cup chopped tomato
¼ cup finely chopped onion
1 (4 ounce) can diced green
chilies

½ cup crushed corn tortilla
chips
4 eggs, beaten until frothy
Salt to taste
½ cup shredded cheddar
cheese

Heat butter in skillet and sauté chopped tomato, onion, and green chilies for 1 minute. Add tortilla chips. Pour eggs into skillet over other ingredients and cook, stirring often, until mixture sets. Sprinkle with salt and cheese.

CHEESY HASH BROWN CASSEROLE

1 (32 ounce) bag frozen
shredded hash browns
2 (10 ounce) cans cream of
potato soup
16 ounces sour cream

2 cups shredded sharp
cheddar cheese
1 cup Parmesan cheese
¼ cup real bacon bits

Combine all ingredients; stir well. Spoon into greased 9x13-inch baking dish. Bake at 350 degrees for 40 minutes or until golden brown.

Every child you encounter is a divine appointment.
WES STAFFORD

• • • • •

*Jesus said, "Let the little children come to me,
and do not hinder them, for the kingdom of
heaven belongs to such as these."*
MATTHEW 19:14 NIV

• • • • •

*Heavenly Father, I praise You that children are so important
to You. As we gather together for dinner tonight, help my
children to feel Your love and care for each one of them. Help
us as parents to increase their understanding of Your feelings
for them. We are so grateful for Your constant presence in our
lives and in our home. Amen.*

BREAKFAST PIZZA

1 tube refrigerated
crescent rolls

1 pound bulk sausage, cooked
and drained

1 cup frozen hash browns,
thawed

1 cup shredded sharp
cheddar cheese

5 eggs

¼ cup milk

½ teaspoon salt

¼ teaspoon pepper

Press rolls in slightly greased 12-inch pizza pan. Seal perforations. Spoon sausage over crust. Sprinkle with hash browns. Top with cheddar cheese. In bowl, beat together remaining ingredients. Pour onto crust. Bake at 375 degrees for 25 to 30 minutes.

· ·

ENGLISH MUFFIN PIZZA

1 English muffin

3 tablespoons spaghetti sauce

¼ cup shredded mozzarella
cheese

4 slices pepperoni

Oregano

Split English muffin and place the two halves on baking sheet. Top each muffin half with half of the sauce, half of the pepperoni, and half of the cheese. Sprinkle with dash of oregano. Bake for 4 to 6 minutes at 350 degrees until cheese is golden brown and bubbly.

BREAKFAST LASAGNA

½ cup sour cream

1 (10 ounce) can cream of mushroom soup

1 (32 ounce) bag frozen shredded hash browns

1 sweet onion, diced

1 pound cooked bacon, diced

1 cup shredded cheddar cheese

1 cup shredded mozzarella cheese

Mix sour cream and mushroom soup until well blended. In lasagna pan, layer hash browns, soup mixture, onions, bacon, and cheese in that order. Cover with foil and bake at 325 degrees for 1 hour. Remove foil and bake 5 minutes longer.

TACO SALAD

1 package taco seasoning

1 pound ground beef, browned and drained

1 small head lettuce, shredded

1 medium onion, diced

1 green pepper, diced

3 small tomatoes, chopped

1 cup shredded cheddar cheese

1 can kidney beans, drained

1 (14 ounce) package tortilla chips, broken

1 bottle ranch dressing with bacon

Mix taco seasoning into ground beef. Cool in refrigerator. Just before serving, mix in remaining ingredients and toss with dressing.

SLOW-COOKER BURRITOS

1 pound ground beef or
    ground pork
2 tablespoons chopped onion
1 can diced and spiced
    tomatoes

1 can refried beans
1 (12 ounce) bag corn tortilla
    chips
1½ cups shredded cheese
    (any kind)

Brown meat and onion; drain. In small bowl, combine tomatoes and beans; blend well. Grease bottom and sides of large slow cooker. Divide ingredients in thirds and start layering. Cover bottom of slow cooker with chips, cover with a third of meat, spread on a third of beans, and sprinkle with a third of cheese. Repeat layers, ending with cheese on top. Cover and cook on low for 4 hours or on high for 2 hours.

CHINESE CHICKEN

1 can crushed pineapple
½ cup water
½ cup vinegar

½ cup brown sugar
Cornstarch
Chicken wings or drumettes

Mix first four ingredients and thicken with cornstarch. Marinate chicken wings or drumettes for 2 hours. Bake at 350 degrees for 45 minutes on foil-lined baking sheet, turning once.

BEEF TIPS WITH NOODLES

2 pounds lean stew meat, cut into bite-sized pieces

1 can cream of mushroom soup

1 package dry onion soup mix

1 cup lemon-lime soda

Cooked noodles or rice

Place meat in 2-quart casserole dish. Top with soup and onion soup mix. Add soda. Do not stir. Cover and bake at 275 degrees for 4 hours. Do not open oven door during cooking. Let stand for 30 minutes before serving.

BAKED PIZZA SANDWICH

2 tablespoons butter, softened

1½ teaspoons Italian
    seasoning

1 teaspoon minced garlic

1 (16 ounce) prepared Italian
    bread shell, sliced in half
    horizontally

4 ounces pepperoni

4 green pepper rings

4 slices tomato

6 slices provolone cheese

Combine butter, Italian seasoning, and garlic in small bowl.
Spread mixture on half of bread shell. Layer with pepperoni,
green pepper, tomato, and cheese. Top with remaining half of
bread shell. Wrap in aluminum foil and place on baking sheet.
Bake at 350 degrees for 18 minutes or until cheese is melted.
Cut into 4 sections and serve warm.

We make a living by what we get;
we make a life by what we give.

WINSTON CHURCHILL

• • • • •

Keep his decrees and commands, which I am giving
you today, so that it may go well with you and your
children after you and that you may live long in the
land the LORD your God gives you for all time.

DEUTERONOMY 4:40 NIV

• • • • •

And in the end, it's not the years in your life
that count. It's the life in your years.

ABRAHAM LINCOLN

VINEYARD CHICKEN SALAD

1 pound boneless, skinless chicken breasts, cooked and finely chopped

1 cup mayonnaise

1 cup grapes, quartered

½ cup chopped dates

1 small can crushed pineapple, drained

1 stalk celery, finely chopped

1 to 1½ teaspoons all-purpose seasoning (low salt)

Combine all ingredients in large bowl, adding more mayonnaise if mixture is too dry. Refrigerate for 2 hours to allow flavors to blend. Serve on bread, croissants, or crackers.

FAMILY BARBECUE BURGERS

4 to 6 hamburger patties

1 cup ketchup

2 tablespoons mustard

½ cup sugar

1 tablespoon vinegar

Grill hamburger patties until done. Combine ketchup, mustard, sugar, and vinegar. Place spoonfuls of mixture in bottom of shallow baking dish; place grilled hamburgers on top. Pour remaining sauce over burgers. Cover and bake at 325 degrees for 1 hour.

PIZZA SPUDS

4 potatoes

½ cup pizza sauce

⅔ cup chopped pepperoni

¼ cup grated Parmesan cheese

¼ cup shredded mozzarella cheese

Poke clean potatoes with fork. Microwave for 6 minutes. Flip and rotate potatoes; microwave 4 to 6 minutes longer. Let stand for 5 minutes. Slice open potatoes. Top with pizza sauce, pepperoni, and cheeses. Microwave for 1 to 2 minutes to melt cheeses.

MEXICAN SANDWICH ROLLS

3 pounds ground beef

1 medium onion, chopped

3 cups shredded cheddar cheese

1 (15 ounce) can tomato sauce

1 (16 ounce) jar salsa

2 dozen hard rolls

Brown ground beef and onion; drain. Add remaining ingredients except rolls. Remove pinch of bread from center of rolls; fill with beef mixture. Wrap each in foil. Bake at 350 degrees for 30 minutes.

BACON CHICKEN

8 slices bacon

4 boneless, skinless chicken
 breasts

1 can condensed cream of
 mushroom soup

¾ cup sour cream

¼ cup flour

Wrap 2 bacon slices around each chicken breast and place in slow cooker. In medium bowl, combine soup, sour cream, and flour; mix thoroughly. Pour over chicken. Cover and cook on low for 7 to 8 hours.

MESSY BUNS

1 to 1½ pounds ground beef

½ cup ketchup

2 tablespoons mustard

2 tablespoons Worcestershire
 sauce

2 tablespoons brown sugar

8 hot dog buns

Brown ground beef in large skillet. Add remaining ingredients except hot dog buns and simmer for 10 minutes. Fill hot dog buns with beef mixture. Serve while hot.

BACON ROLL-UPS

1 package chicken
   stuffing mix

1 cup chicken broth, undiluted

1 (12 ounce) package bacon

Mix stuffing and chicken broth. Cut bacon slices in half. Spoon stuffing mixture onto each bacon half; roll up and secure with toothpick. Place on broiler pan and bake at 350 degrees for 30 minutes. Serve hot.

FOUR-LAYER BREAKFAST DISH

1 pound ground sausage

4 eggs

¼ cup milk

1 tube refrigerated crescent
   rolls

2 to 3 cups shredded
   mozzarella cheese

Preheat oven to 350 degrees. Brown sausage; drain. Beat eggs and milk. Press crescent roll dough in bottom of buttered 9x13-inch casserole dish; layer sausage and egg mixture and top with cheese. Bake for 30 to 50 minutes or until eggs are not runny.

 ## GIVING TO OTHERS

Preparing food for people who need it is a great way to involve your family in sharing with others. Consider preparing snacks to take to a nursing home or volunteering to provide a meal for a local homeless shelter. As a family, help to distribute this food to others, and remember these people in your family prayer time.

Heavenly Father, we thank You for all of our blessings. We remember our neighbors in need right now. Please give us the desire to share our blessings with others so that we might be Your hands and feet as we share our daily bread with those who need it more than we do.

· · · · ·

Christ has no body on earth but yours, no hands but yours, no feet but yours. Yours are the eyes through which Christ's compassion for the world is to look out; yours are the feet with which He is to go about doing good; and yours are the hands with which He is to bless us now.

SAINT TERESA OF AVILA

MICROWAVE SPANISH RICE

6 slices bacon, cooked and
   crumbled; reserve drippings

1 medium onion, chopped

1 cup minute rice, uncooked

1 (16 ounce) can tomatoes,
   undrained

1 cup tomato juice

¼ cup chopped green
   bell pepper

1 tablespoon chopped
   fresh parsley

¼ teaspoon pepper

¼ teaspoon salt

Pour bacon drippings into microwavable bowl; add onion
and rice. Microwave on high for 3 to 4 minutes or until lightly
browned. Stir in remaining ingredients and cooked bacon.
Cover and microwave on high for 8 minutes or until rice is
tender.

MICROWAVE CHICKEN LASAGNA

¼ cup chopped cilantro

½ cup chopped onion

2 cups shredded cheddar cheese, divided

1 (28 ounce) can enchilada sauce, divided

12 tortillas

8 ounces cream cheese, softened

3 cups shredded cooked chicken

Mix cilantro, onion, and 1 cup cheddar cheese. Spread ⅔ cup enchilada sauce in microwavable dish. Pour remaining sauce into large bowl. Dip 4 tortillas into sauce and arrange in microwavable baking dish. Spread one-third of cream cheese over tortillas. Top with 1 cup chicken. Repeat layers twice. Top with remaining sauce and cheddar cheese. Cover and microwave on high for 13 minutes or until heated through.

CHEESY BEEF-A-RONI

1 pound ground beef, browned
1 (15 ounce) can sloppy joe
  sauce

¾ cup elbow macaroni, cooked
1 cup shredded cheese
  (any kind)

In large skillet, add first three ingredients and simmer 5 minutes or until heated through. Top with cheese.

. . . .

TURKEY QUESADILLAS

4 flour tortillas
4 teaspoons butter
Dijon mustard

8 slices deli turkey
2 cups shredded cheddar
  jack cheese

Spread one side of each tortilla with 1 teaspoon butter. Spread mustard on other side. Add 2 turkey slices and top with ½ cup cheese. Fold in half. Place quesadillas, buttered side down, in nonstick skillet. Cook 1 minute on each side or until golden brown.

SUNDAY BRUNCH CASSEROLE

½ pound sliced bacon

½ cup chopped onion

½ cup chopped green pepper

12 eggs

1 cup milk

16 ounces frozen hash browns, thawed

1 cup shredded cheddar cheese

1 teaspoon salt

½ teaspoon pepper

Cook bacon in skillet until crisp. Remove from pan with slotted spoon; crumble and set aside. In bacon drippings, sauté onion and green pepper until tender; remove with slotted spoon. Beat eggs and milk in large bowl; stir in hash browns, cheese, salt, pepper, onion, green pepper, and bacon. Place in greased baking dish. Bake uncovered at 350 degrees for 35 to 45 minutes.

PIZZA POCKETS

1 pound ground sausage, browned

1 cup spaghetti sauce

1 teaspoon oregano

½ teaspoon pepper

1 pinch salt

1 cup shredded mozzarella cheese

1 (8 ounce) tube refrigerated pizza dough

Mix all ingredients together except dough. Divide dough into fourths. Spoon one-quarter of mixture into each pocket and fold over, sealing edges firmly with fork. Place on ungreased baking sheet. Bake at 350 degrees for 15 to 20 minutes or until golden brown.

SODA POP CHICKEN

1 cup cola

1 cup prepared barbecue sauce

1½ pounds boneless, skinless chicken breast pieces

Mix cola and barbecue sauce in large saucepan or dutch oven. Add chicken. Cover and cook over medium heat for 45 minutes or until chicken is tender and no longer pink. Serve with rice.

BOWTIE MARINARA

16 ounces bowtie pasta

1 pound lean ground beef

1 (24 ounce) jar spaghetti sauce

2 cups shredded mozzarella cheese

Prepare pasta according to package directions. Brown beef and drain. Add pasta and spaghetti sauce and heat through. Top with cheese.

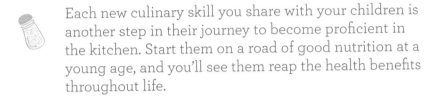

KIDS IN THE KITCHEN

Each new culinary skill you share with your children is another step in their journey to become proficient in the kitchen. Start them on a road of good nutrition at a young age, and you'll see them reap the health benefits throughout life.

Have your children create and decorate signs as a reminder to always wash hands before handling food. Post one near your kitchen sink and one in the bathroom.

Consider using plastic measuring cups and mixing bowls when your child helps in the kitchen. These are lighter than glass tools and are less likely to break.

To prepare for each new recipe, read through the ingredients and directions with your kids and explain any new words or kitchen techniques. Soon you'll have a miniature chef in your kitchen!

Assign each child a special task each time you cook or bake together. Have fruit or vegetables to wash? Crown one child prince (or princess) of produce and address him as "Your Highness." Get creative as you assign tasks like stirring, pouring, measuring, and cleaning up afterward.

As kids grow and mature, you'll be able to give them more diverse tasks in the kitchen. Start by teaching safe and easy tasks like how to mix with a wooden spoon, add ingredients, and clean up the workspace. Always supervise, especially when a new skill is being learned, and offer positive reinforcement when the skill is mastered.

HAM ROLLS

½ cup margarine

½ tablespoon poppy seeds

½ teaspoon Worcestershire sauce

½ tablespoon mustard

½ tablespoon onion flakes or minced onion

1 tube refrigerated biscuits

Baked and sliced ham

Shredded swiss or mozzarella cheese

Melt margarine and stir in poppy seeds, Worcestershire sauce, mustard, and onion; set aside. Top biscuits with ham. Pour margarine mixture over ham, sprinkle with cheese, and let set overnight. Bake at 350 degrees for 15 to 20 minutes or until cheese is melted.

. . . .

HAM 'N' CHEESE PIE

1½ cups cubed fully cooked ham

1 cup shredded cheddar cheese

¼ cup chopped sweet onion

½ cup baking mix

1 cup milk

¼ teaspoon salt

⅛ teaspoon pepper

2 eggs

Sprinkle ham, cheese, and onion in greased 9-inch pie plate. Mix remaining ingredients and pour into pie plate. Bake at 400 degrees for 35 minutes or until knife inserted in center comes out clean. Cool 5 minutes. Garnish with sliced tomatoes if desired.

CHEESEBURGER AND FRIES CASSEROLE

1 pound frozen french fries, baked according to package directions

1 pound ground beef, browned

1 (14 ounce) can sloppy joe sauce

2 cups shredded cheddar cheese

Place prepared fries in bottom of 9x13-inch casserole dish. Spoon browned ground beef on top of fries. Add sloppy joe sauce. Top with cheese. Bake at 350 degrees for 30 minutes or until heated through.

. . . .

BAKED SAUSAGE CASSEROLE

12 slices white bread, cubed

1 pound sausage, cooked and drained

1 cup shredded cheddar cheese

6 eggs

2 cups milk

1 teaspoon salt

½ teaspoon pepper

Evenly sprinkle cubed bread in greased 9x13-inch pan. Spoon meat over bread and top with cheese. In separate bowl, beat eggs, milk, salt, and pepper. Pour over bread mixture. Bake at 350 degrees for 20 to 25 minutes or until done.

PORCUPINE MEATBALLS

2 pounds ground beef
2 (11 ounce) cans tomato soup
1 teaspoon chili powder
Salt and pepper to taste

1 egg
1 medium onion, finely
   chopped
¼ cup rice (not instant)
1½ teaspoons chili powder

In skillet, brown ground beef and set aside. Heat soup to boil and then reduce to simmer. With each can of soup, add 2 cans water. Add to soup: 1 teaspoon chili powder and salt and pepper to taste. Let soup mixture simmer while mixing the following ingredients in large bowl: egg, onion, rice, remaining chili powder, and ground beef. Salt and pepper to taste. Mix well and shape into meatballs. Be careful not to pack meatballs too tightly. Drop meatballs into hot soup mixture and bring to boil. Reduce heat and simmer for 1½ hours.

CRESCENT ROLL CHICKEN

1 can cream of chicken soup

½ cup shredded cheddar cheese

½ cup milk

1 tube refrigerated crescent rolls

3 boneless, skinless chicken breasts, cooked and cut into small pieces

Combine soup, cheese, and milk. Pour half in 9x13-inch pan. Separate crescent rolls. Place as much cut-up chicken in each roll as will fit; roll up, tucking in edges. Place in pan. Spoon remaining sauce over rolls. If desired, sprinkle cheese over all. Bake at 350 degrees for 25 to 30 minutes or until lightly browned. *Note:* If using 29-ounce can of condensed cream of chicken soup, use more cheese and 2 tubes of crescent rolls.

BACON AND POTATO CASSEROLE

4 cups frozen shredded hash brown potatoes

½ cup finely chopped onion

8 ounces bacon, cooked and crumbled

1 cup shredded cheddar cheese

1 (12 ounce) can evaporated milk

1 large egg, lightly beaten

1 teaspoon seasoned salt

¼ teaspoon pepper

Layer half of potatoes, half of onion, half of bacon, and half of cheese in greased 8-inch baking dish; repeat layers. Combine evaporated milk, egg, seasoned salt, and pepper in small bowl. Pour evenly over potato mixture. Cover and bake for 55 to 60 minutes at 350 degrees. Uncover and bake for 5 more minutes. Let stand for 10 minutes before serving.

VEGETABLE ROLL-UPS

1 (8 ounce) package
  cream cheese

1 (8 ounce) container
  sour cream

1 cup shredded
  cheddar cheese

1 package dry ranch
  dressing mix

1 cup chopped broccoli

1 cup chopped cauliflower

½ cup chopped carrots

½ cup chopped onion

Flour tortillas

Mix all ingredients and spread on tortillas. Roll up tightly and
wrap in plastic wrap. Refrigerate overnight. When ready to
serve, unwrap and slice into pinwheels.

QUICK 'N' EASY ENCHILADAS

1 (10 ounce) can Swanson
   premium chicken
2 cups shredded Mexican-style
   cheese, divided

1 (24 ounce) jar salsa, divided
8 flour tortillas

Drain and shred chicken. Mix with 1 cup cheese and 1½ to 2 cups salsa. Spoon ¼ cup mixture down center of each tortilla; roll tortillas and place seam side down in 7x11-inch baking dish. Evenly spread remaining salsa over tortillas. Sprinkle with remaining cheese. Bake at 350 degrees for 30 minutes.

MARZETTI

1½ teaspoons vegetable oil, divided

1 teaspoon garlic powder

1 pound ground beef

1 (12 ounce) can tomato paste

Water

1 teaspoon oregano

2 teaspoons sugar

2 teaspoons parsley flakes

2 cups elbow macaroni, uncooked

2 cups shredded mozzarella cheese

Heat 1 teaspoon vegetable oil in skillet; add garlic powder. Brown ground beef in oil; drain. Reduce heat to low and add tomato paste; fill empty can with water and add to skillet. Add additional can of water and stir. Stir in oregano, sugar, and parsley flakes. Simmer for 20 minutes, stirring occasionally. Boil macaroni in salted water with ½ teaspoon vegetable oil; drain and add to beef mixture. Add mozzarella and let melt; stir thoroughly.

BREAKFAST CASSEROLE

2 tubes refrigerated
   crescent rolls

1 small onion, chopped

1 green pepper, chopped

½ cup mushrooms

2 tablespoons butter

8 eggs

1 package sausage links,
   browned and sliced

2 cups shredded cheddar
   cheese

Press crescent roll dough into 9x13-inch pan, pressing halfway
up sides. Sauté onions, green peppers, and mushrooms in
butter. Set aside. In same saucepan, scramble eggs. Layer eggs,
vegetable mixture, sausage, and cheese on top of crescent roll
crust. Bake as directed on crescent roll package, or until done.

TATER TOT CASSEROLE

1 pound ground beef, browned
½ cup frozen peas
½ cup frozen corn
1 (10 ounce) can cream of
    potato soup

1 (10 ounce) can cream of
    onion soup
2 cups shredded sharp
    cheddar cheese, divided
4 cups frozen tater tots

In 9x13-inch casserole dish, mix beef, peas, corn, soups, and
1 cup cheese. Top with tater tots and bake at 350 degrees for
45 minutes or until tots begin to brown. Sprinkle remaining
cheese over top and bake for 5 more minutes or until cheese
melts.

NOT-TOO-HOT CHILI

1 pound ground beef

1 cup chopped onion

4 minced garlic cloves

1 cup chopped green pepper

2 (14 ounce) cans diced
   tomatoes

1 (8 ounce) can tomato sauce

1½ tablespoons chili powder

1 teaspoon salt

¼ teaspoon cayenne pepper

¼ teaspoon paprika

¼ teaspoon cumin

1 (15½ ounce) can kidney
   beans, drained

Brown ground beef with onion, garlic, and green pepper in large skillet. Drain fat and transfer to slow cooker. Stir in remaining ingredients and cook on high for 2 hours, stirring occasionally. Refrigerate 24 hours. Reheat in microwave or on stovetop. Serve topped with your favorite chili toppings.

TUNA SHELLS

8 jumbo pasta shells, cooked and drained

1 cup tuna salad

½ cup shredded cheddar cheese

Fill each shell with tuna salad and sprinkle with cheese. Store in refrigerator. Makes a great after-school snack.

CHEESY CRESCENT DOGS

1 tube refrigerated crescent rolls

4 reduced-fat hot dogs, cut in half

4 slices cheddar cheese

Unroll crescent roll dough. Add a hot dog half and ½ slice of cheese to each roll. Roll up and pinch seams. Place on greased baking sheet. Bake as package directs.

KIDS' "PICK THE THEME" NIGHT

Have your kids plan a special themed dinner for your family. Allow them to do as much as they can on their own. They can invite a set number of family and friends.

 The evening could center around a cuisine type (Mexican, Italian, all-American), a color (green eggs and ham, anyone?), or a letter of the alphabet (a B meal could be made up of burgers, beans, baked apples, and brownies for dessert).

 Help them choose a game to go along with their theme.

 Have them create special invitations and decorations.

 Allow them to choose the recipes and create a shopping list.

 Help them make their purchases and prepare the meal, letting them do most of the work.

Children are a gift from the LORD;
they are a reward from him.

PSALM 127:3 NLT

BUBBLE-UP TACO PIZZA

2 (16 ounce) tubes refrigerated buttermilk biscuits

1½ pounds lean ground beef, browned with 1 tablespoon taco seasoning

2 cups shredded Colby/ Monterey Jack cheese

2 cups shredded lettuce

1 small tomato, diced

Salsa

Snip biscuits into fourths and drop evenly into greased 9x13-inch baking pan. Spread meat mixture evenly over biscuits. Sprinkle cheese over meat. Bake at 350 degrees for about 25 minutes or until biscuits are done in middle. Immediately cover with lettuce and tomato. Drizzle salsa over top and serve.

EASY BEAN ENCHILADAS

1 (16 ounce) jar salsa

1 (16 ounce) can refried beans

1 (10 ounce) can red enchilada
   sauce

½ cup sliced black olives

10 corn tortillas, sliced in half,
   divided

2 cups shredded cheddar
   cheese, divided

In saucepan, bring salsa, beans, enchilada sauce, and olives to a boil. Reduce heat to low and cook for 5 minutes, stirring constantly. Layer half of tortillas on bottom of greased 9x13-inch baking dish. Cover with half of bean mix; sprinkle with 1 cup cheese. Repeat layers once. Bake, covered, for 25 minutes at 375 degrees. Remove cover during last 5 minutes.

CHEESY TACO CASSEROLE

1 (16 ounce) jar chunky salsa

1 (10 ounce) can red enchilada sauce

1 pound lean ground beef, browned with 1 small chopped onion

12 taco shells, broken into pieces

1½ cups shredded cheddar cheese, divided

Sour cream, for garnish

In skillet, add salsa and enchilada sauce to beef and onion. Bring to a boil. Reduce heat to low; cook, stirring frequently, for 4 minutes. Layer half of taco shell pieces in ungreased 9x13-inch baking dish. Top with half of beef mixture and half of cheese. Repeat layers once. Bake at 350 degrees for 15 minutes. Garnish with sour cream.

BEEF TACO BAKE

1 small sweet onion, chopped

1 (10 ounce) can tomato soup

1 cup salsa

½ cup water

8 corn tortillas, cut into
    1-inch pieces

1 pound ground beef, browned
    and drained

1 cup shredded cheddar
    cheese, divided

Add onion, soup, salsa, water, and tortilla pieces to beef. Add half of cheese and mix well. Spoon into baking dish and cover. Bake at 400 degrees for 30 minutes. Sprinkle with remaining cheese.

CRUNCHY TACOS

1 pound ground beef

1 tablespoon chili powder

1 cup salsa, plus extra for serving

8 taco shells

1 cup shredded lettuce

1 cup shredded cheddar cheese

Sour cream

Cook beef and chili powder in skillet until browned. Drain. Add salsa and heat through. Spoon about ¼ cup meat mixture into each taco shell. Top with lettuce and cheese. Serve with additional salsa and sour cream.

FAVORITE CLASSICS

Finally, brothers and sisters, whatever is true, whatever is noble, whatever is right, whatever is pure, whatever is lovely, whatever is admirable— if anything is excellent or praiseworthy— think about such things.

PHILIPPIANS 4:8

HAMBURGER STROGANOFF

1 pound ground beef

½ cup chopped onion

¼ cup butter

2 tablespoons flour

¼ teaspoon pepper

1 teaspoon salt

1 teaspoon garlic salt

1 (8 ounce) can mushrooms, drained

1 (10½ ounce) can cream of chicken soup

1 cup sour cream

2 cups hot cooked noodles

Heat ground beef, onion, and butter in large skillet on medium-high heat until onion is tender. Stir in flour, pepper, salt, garlic salt, and mushrooms. Cook, stirring constantly, for 5 minutes. Remove from heat and stir in soup. Simmer for 10 minutes uncovered. Stir in sour cream and serve over hot noodles.

FAST FISH DINNER

14 ounces frozen batter-dipped fish

1 (16 ounce) package frozen french fries

1 (10 ounce) can cream of celery soup

¾ cup milk

⅓ cup mayonnaise

2 tablespoons relish

Place fish on bottom of greased baking dish. Add french fries. Mix remaining ingredients together. Pour over casserole, covering all french fries and fish. Bake at 350 degrees for 45 minutes or until bubbly.

. . . .

BOB'S BAKED BEANS

4 slices bacon, cooked and crumbled

1 small sweet onion, chopped

1 (26 ounce) can vegetarian baked beans

⅓ cup ketchup

2 tablespoons brown sugar

½ teaspoon Worcestershire sauce

Combine all ingredients and pour into casserole dish. Bake at 350 degrees for 30 minutes.

 A LONDON EVENING

 Prepare a traditional English "fish and chips" dinner or use the recipe on page 51.

 Make the Strawberry Trifle (found on page 176) for dessert.

 Play a few traditional English games as a family: London Bridge, Hopscotch, Simon Says.

 Discuss our history with England. Check out a history book at the library and take turns reading from it and looking at the pictures. Are your ancestors from England? Discuss what you know of your heritage and how you are or aren't connected to the country.

 There are many family-friendly movies set in England. Choose one that best suits your children's ages. Consider the following: *101 Dalmatians*, *Garfield: A Tale of Two Kitties*, *Mary Poppins*, *Chronicles of Narnia*.

 Pinterest is a great tool to find theme night and family dinner ideas! Follow my "A London Evening" board at http://pinterest.com/marileeparrish/a-london-evening/.

SPEEDY BEEFY STROGANOFF

1½ pounds ground beef

1 medium onion, chopped

2 cans condensed cheddar cheese soup

1 can sliced mushrooms with juice

Salt and pepper to taste

In large skillet, brown ground beef and onion; drain. Stir in soup and mushrooms with juice. Season to taste. Simmer until heated through. Serve over noodles, rice, or toast.

. . . .

SKILLET HAM AND POTATOES

2 tablespoons butter

1½ cups frozen shredded hash browns

½ pound ham, diced

Shredded cheese (any kind)

Melt butter in skillet. Add hash browns and cook over medium heat for about 10 minutes, making sure not to let hash browns stick to bottom of pan. Add ham. Top with cheese. Reduce heat to low and cover until cheese is melted.

BEEF TIPS WITH GRAVY

1 pound round steak

2 tablespoons oil

1 (10½ ounce) can cream of mushroom soup

1 envelope onion soup mix

Cut meat into 1½-inch strips; in skillet, brown strips in oil over medium-high heat. Mix mushroom soup with 2 cups water. Add to browned meat. Stir in onion soup mix and simmer for 1 hour. Serve over noodles or rice.

. . . .

CHICKEN AND RICE

6 chicken breast halves

1 cup fresh mushrooms

1 cup cider vinegar

1 (10½ ounce) can cream of mushroom soup

1 pint sour cream

Dash paprika

Preheat oven to 350 degrees. Debone chicken breasts and arrange in baking dish. Bake for 15 minutes. Chop mushrooms and combine in bowl with remaining ingredients except paprika. Pour over chicken and bake for 30 minutes. Sprinkle with paprika and serve over white rice.

FAMILY ROAST

1 (5 pound) rump roast

3 (10 ounce) cans golden mushroom soup

½ cup water

4 small onions, chopped in large chunks

16 carrots, peeled and sliced

10 medium potatoes

Salt and pepper to taste

In baking pan, place roast, soup, water, and vegetables; add salt and pepper to taste. Cover and bake at 350 degrees. Check roast after 2 hours. Continue baking until tender.

DINNER CONVERSATION STARTERS

Pick one of the following questions to ask at the beginning of a meal.

 What was your favorite and least favorite thing that happened today and why?

 What do you wish we would do more of as a family? Why?

 What do you wish we would do less of as a family? Why?

 Where should we go on vacation this year?

 What ministry activities can we get involved in as a family?

 If we were to take a family mission trip, how would you feel about that?

 Do you have a friend who is struggling right now? How can we help or pray for him or her?

 Do you feel valued in our family? Why or why not?

 What is your favorite class at school? Tell us about it.

 Who is your favorite teacher or church leader? What is it you like about him or her?

CHICKEN SKILLET

4 cups frozen diced hash brown potatoes

1 cup chopped onion

½ cup chopped green bell pepper

½ cup chopped red bell pepper

3 tablespoons oil

2 cups diced cooked chicken

1 cup half-and-half

2 chicken bouillon cubes

2 teaspoons flour

¼ teaspoon pepper

1 cup shredded sharp cheddar cheese

Cook potatoes, onion, and bell peppers in large skillet with oil for 13 minutes or until potatoes are cooked. Sprinkle chicken over potatoes. In small saucepan, combine remaining ingredients except cheese. Cook for 4 minutes over medium heat, stirring constantly until mixture thickens. Pour over chicken. Top with cheese.

CRUNCHY LUNCH CASSEROLE

½ cup chopped celery
½ cup chopped onion
½ cup cashew pieces
1 cup chow mein noodles

1 (5 ounce) can tuna, drained
1 (10 ounce) can cream of
  mushroom soup
¼ cup water

Combine all ingredients in casserole dish. Bake for 15 to 20 minutes at 375 degrees.

· ·

CHICKEN TACOS

1 tablespoon olive oil
1 small sweet onion, chopped
½ teaspoon chili powder
1 (10 ounce) can nacho cheese
  soup

2 (5 ounce) cans chunk
  chicken, drained
8 taco shells
Shredded lettuce
Salsa

Heat oil in skillet. Add onion and chili powder and cook for 1 minute. Add soup and chicken. Heat through, about 4 to 5 minutes. Fill taco shells with mixture. Top with lettuce and salsa.

MEATBALL SUBS

3 frozen, precooked meatballs
   per sandwich

2 tablespoons spaghetti sauce
   per sandwich, warmed

Hot dog buns

Shredded mozzarella cheese

Warm meatballs in microwave according to package directions.
Put 3 meatballs in a hot dog bun. Top with warm sauce and
sprinkle with cheese.

. . . .

ITALIAN SAUSAGE SANDWICH

1 small sweet onion, sliced

1 green bell pepper, sliced

1 red bell pepper, sliced

2 tablespoons butter

2 precooked Italian sausage
   links per sandwich

Hot dog buns

Provolone cheese slices

Sauté onion and peppers in butter. Add sausage links and heat
until warmed through. Place 2 sausage links in a hot dog bun.
Add as many onions and peppers as you like. Top with 1 slice of
provolone cheese. Place on cookie sheet and broil on low until
cheese is melted.

CORNED BEEF SANDWICH

1 (12 ounce) can corned beef
2 small onions, finely chopped
4 stalks celery, finely chopped

4 teaspoons mayonnaise
½ pound processed cheese, cut into small cubes
12 buns

Combine first five ingredients, fill buns, and wrap each bun in foil. Heat sandwiches at 350 degrees for 15 minutes.

. . . .

DELI STROMBOLI

1 (13.8 ounce) tube refrigerated pizza crust
1 tablespoon Dijon mustard
1 tablespoon real mayonnaise

¼ pound deli corned beef
¼ pound deli turkey breast
¼ pound sliced swiss cheese

On cookie sheet, unfold pizza crust and flatten into large rectangle. Spread mustard and mayo over crust. Layer deli meats and cheese evenly over crust. Roll up and pinch seams. Cut slit in top for steam to escape. Bake at 400 degrees for 15 to 18 minutes or until golden brown.

CLASSIC POTATO SALAD

1 cup mayonnaise
2 tablespoons vinegar
1 teaspoon sugar
1½ teaspoons salt
¼ teaspoon pepper

4 cups potatoes, boiled and cubed
1 cup sliced celery
½ cup chopped onion
2 hard-boiled eggs, chopped

Blend mayonnaise, vinegar, sugar, salt, and pepper; pour over mixture of potatoes, celery, onion, and eggs. Refrigerate until ready to serve.

· ·

BAKED CHEESY POTATOES

1 (2 pound) package frozen hash browns
1 can condensed cream of potato soup
1 can condensed cream of celery soup

1½ cups sour cream
1½ cup chopped onion
Salt and pepper to taste
1 cup shredded cheddar cheese, divided

Place hash browns in large baking dish. Mix potato soup, celery soup, sour cream, onion, salt and pepper to taste, and ½ cup cheese. Pour mixture over hash browns; sprinkle with remaining ½ cup cheese. Bake at 350 degrees for 1 hour.

STUFFED PEPPERS

3 to 4 pounds ground beef

2 to 3 eggs

1 cup white rice, uncooked

1 small onion, chopped

1 cup shredded cheddar
   cheese

¼ teaspoon salt

¼ teaspoon pepper

5 to 6 large green peppers

3 to 4 large cans condensed
   tomato soup

Water

Mix ground beef, eggs, rice, onion, cheese, salt, and pepper; stuff into cleaned, hollowed-out green peppers. Place in large soup pan with tomato soup and 3 to 4 soup cans full of water. Cook over medium-high heat, boiling slowly for 3 hours. Serve with mashed potatoes.

SUPER-EASY CHICKEN TETRAZZINI

¼ cup butter

1 can condensed cream of
mushroom soup

¼ teaspoon garlic salt

⅛ teaspoon pepper

2 chicken bouillon cubes

¼ cup water

8 ounces spaghetti, cooked
and drained

8 ounces boneless, skinless
chicken, cooked and cubed

2 ounces shredded Parmesan
cheese

Melt butter in large skillet. Add soup, garlic salt, pepper, bouillon, and water. Bring to a boil, stirring constantly. Add spaghetti and chicken; stir gently but thoroughly. Pour mixture into casserole dish. Sprinkle with cheese. Cover and bake at 400 degrees for 20 minutes.

TACO BAKE

1 pound ground beef

1 can condensed tomato soup

1 cup salsa

½ cup milk

6 medium flour tortillas, cut into 1-inch strips

1 cup shredded Colby/ Monterey Jack cheese, divided

Brown ground beef; drain. Add soup, salsa, milk, tortilla strips, and ½ cup cheese. Pour mixture into 2-quart casserole dish and cover. Bake at 400 degrees for 30 minutes. Remove from oven and sprinkle with remaining cheese before serving.

CHICKEN FAJITAS

1 pound boneless, skinless chicken breasts, cut into strips

1 can diced tomatoes

1 can diced green chilies

1 small onion, chopped

2 green bell peppers, sliced

1 package fajita seasoning

Layer ingredients in order given in large slow cooker. Cook on high until juices boil. Cook on low for 4 hours or until chicken is tender. Serve over cooked rice or in tortilla shells.

EGG CASSEROLE

Butter

6 slices bread, cubed

1 pound bulk sausage, browned, drained, and crumbled

8 ounces shredded sharp cheddar cheese

8 to 12 large eggs, beaten

1 teaspoon dry mustard

2 cups half-and-half

Bacon strips, cooked (optional)

Grease 9x13-inch baking dish with butter. Layer bread, sausage, and cheese in dish. Mix beaten eggs with mustard and half-and-half. Pour egg mixture over layers in dish. Refrigerate uncovered overnight. Bake uncovered at 350 degrees for 30 to 35 minutes. If desired, add cooked bacon strips to top of casserole 5 minutes before baking time is complete.

FIVE-INGREDIENT ONE-DISH MEAL

1 pound ground beef

1 can cut green beans, drained

1 can whole-kernel corn, drained

1 can condensed cream of mushroom soup

4 cups mashed potatoes, prepared

Brown ground beef; drain. In 2-quart casserole dish, combine beef, beans, corn, and soup. Cover with mashed potatoes. Bake at 375 degrees for 25 to 30 minutes or until browned and heated through.

. . . .

45-MINUTE CASSEROLE

1 pound ground beef

1 large onion, chopped

1 can condensed cream of celery soup

1 small can sauerkraut

1 bag frozen tater tots

Brown ground beef and onion; drain. Place in casserole dish. Top with soup. Drain and rinse sauerkraut; spread over casserole mixture. Place tater tots over all. Bake at 350 degrees for 45 minutes.

She is clothed with strength and dignity;
she can laugh at the days to come.
She speaks with wisdom,
and faithful instruction is on her tongue.
She watches over the affairs of her household
and does not eat the bread of idleness.
Her children arise and call her blessed;
her husband also, and he praises her:
"Many women do noble things,
but you surpass them all."

PROVERBS 31:25–29 NIV

• • • • •

Dear Lord, please help me to build my home with wisdom.
Forgive me when I envy others instead of being thankful for
my own family and the life in which You have abundantly
blessed me! Help me to be more understanding and loving in
my family relationships.

SLOW-COOKER MAC 'N' CHEESE

1 (16 ounce) box elbow
    macaroni

1 tablespoon vegetable oil

1 (13 ounce) can evaporated
    milk

1½ cups milk

4½ cups shredded cheddar
    cheese, divided

½ cup melted butter

Cook macaroni according to package directions; drain.
Grease bottom and sides of slow cooker. Place hot macaroni
and vegetable oil in slow cooker; add remaining ingredients,
reserving ½ cup cheese. Stir gently to combine. Cover and
cook on low for 3 to 4 hours, stirring occasionally. Just before
serving, sprinkle with remaining cheese.

TUNA NOODLE CASSEROLE

1 can condensed cream of
   mushroom soup

½ cup milk

1 cup peas, cooked

2 (6 ounce) cans tuna, drained
   and flaked

2 cups egg noodles, cooked

2 tablespoons dry bread
   crumbs

1 tablespoon margarine,
   melted

Mix soup, milk, peas, tuna, and egg noodles in 1½-quart
casserole dish. Bake at 400 degrees for 20 minutes. Stir. Mix
bread crumbs with margarine and sprinkle on top of casserole.
Bake 5 minutes longer before serving.

BARBECUED SPARERIBS

1 rack ribs

1 large onion, sliced

1 lemon, sliced

1 cup ketchup

⅓ cup Worcestershire sauce

1 teaspoon chili sauce

1 teaspoon salt

2 dashes hot sauce

2 cups water

Place ribs in shallow baking pan, meaty side up. On each individual rib, place 1 slice of onion and 1 slice of lemon. Roast at 450 degrees for 30 minutes. Combine remaining ingredients in medium saucepan and bring to a boil; pour over ribs. Continue baking for 45 minutes to 1 hour.

POPPY SEED CHICKEN

2 cans condensed cream of
  chicken soup

1 (8 ounce) container sour
  cream

4 boneless, skinless chicken
  breasts, cooked and cubed

1 small box butter-flavored
  crackers, crushed

2 teaspoons poppy seeds

½ cup butter, melted

In large bowl, blend soup and sour cream; add chicken. Place
in casserole dish. Top with crushed crackers and sprinkle with
poppy seeds. Pour melted butter over all. Bake at 350 degrees
for 30 minutes. Serve over rice, potatoes, toast, or biscuits.

COUNTRY-STYLE SCALLOPED POTATOES 'N' HAM

8 red potatoes, thinly sliced
  (skin on)
1½ pounds ham, cubed
¼ cup flour

Whole milk
4 tablespoons butter
Pepper to taste

Place potatoes and ham in deep baking dish; mix well. Add flour and enough milk to cover mixture; stir. Top with butter and pepper to taste. Bake at 350 degrees for 1½ hours or until potatoes reach desired tenderness.

PARMESAN CHICKEN DINNER

2 cloves garlic, minced

¼ cup zesty Italian dressing

4 small boneless, skinless chicken breasts

¼ teaspoon black pepper

1 teaspoon basil, divided

1 (10 ounce) package frozen mixed vegetables, thawed

1 teaspoon salt

2 tablespoons grated Parmesan cheese

Cook garlic and dressing together in large skillet on medium heat for 1 minute. Add chicken and season with pepper and ¾ teaspoon basil. Cook 5 minutes on each side or until chicken is no longer pink. Add vegetables to skillet and sprinkle with remaining basil and salt. Cook for 3 more minutes, stirring occasionally. Top with cheese. Serve alone or with pasta.

CREAM CHEESE 'N' BEAN CHICKEN

4 boneless, skinless chicken breasts, frozen

1 (15½ ounce) can black beans, drained

1 (15 ounce) jar salsa

1 (8 ounce) package cream cheese

Place frozen chicken breasts in slow cooker. Add black beans and salsa. Cook on high for about 5 hours. Toss block of cream cheese on top and let stand for 30 minutes.

. . . .

MOM'S CHILI

2 to 3 pounds ground beef

3 large cans condensed tomato soup

Water

2 large cans kidney beans

1 (12 ounce) can tomato paste

Chili powder to taste

Brown ground beef; drain. In large saucepan, mix beef with tomato soup and 3 soup cans of water. Drain kidney beans; add to ground beef mixture. Add tomato paste (to thicken soup). Add chili powder to taste. Cook over medium heat for 30 to 45 minutes.

DELICIOUS SLOW-COOKED BEEF SANDWICHES

2 pounds beef stew meat

1 can condensed cream of celery soup

1 can condensed cream of mushroom soup

½ package dry onion soup mix

Buns or bread

Rinse stew meat and place in slow cooker. Add remaining ingredients except buns; stir. Reduce heat to low and let cook overnight. Beef will become shredded as it cooks. Enjoy on buns or other bread of your choice.

. . . .

CREAMY MUSHROOM PORK CHOPS

3 potatoes, peeled and sliced

4 pork chops

Salt and pepper to taste

2 cans condensed cream of mushroom soup

Slice potatoes and place in bottom of slow cooker. Season pork chops with salt and pepper; place on top of potatoes. Cover chops with soup and cook on low for 8 hours.

CLASSIC GREEN BEAN BAKE

1 can condensed cream of
  mushroom soup

½ cup milk

1 teaspoon soy sauce

Dash pepper

4 cups cut green beans,
  cooked

1 (2.8 ounce) can french-fried
  onions, divided

Combine soup, milk, soy sauce, and pepper in 1½-quart casserole dish. Stir in beans and half of onions. Bake at 350 degrees for about 25 minutes or until hot. Stir mixture and top with remaining onions. Bake 5 minutes longer.

· ·

BAKED CORN

1 can cream-style corn

1 can whole-kernel corn,
  drained

2 eggs

1 cup sour cream

1 box corn muffin mix

½ cup margarine

Mix all ingredients except margarine; pour into baking dish. Melt margarine and pour over corn mixture. Bake at 350 degrees for 30 to 40 minutes.

LEMON CHICKEN AND BROCCOLI

1 tablespoon butter

4 to 5 boneless, skinless
chicken breasts

2 cups broccoli florets

1 cup chicken broth

Juice of 1 lemon

Melt butter in 9x13-inch baking dish by placing in preheated oven for a few minutes. Add chicken and broccoli. Add chicken broth and then lemon juice. Bake uncovered at 400 degrees for 35 to 40 minutes.

. . . .

15-MINUTE CREAMY FETTUCCINE ALFREDO

1 (8 ounce) package cream
cheese, cubed

½ cup margarine

¾ cup grated Parmesan
cheese

½ cup milk

8 ounces fettuccine pasta,
cooked

1 cup frozen peas, thawed
(optional)

1 cup cubed ham (optional)

In large saucepan, combine first four ingredients. Cook over low heat, stirring until smooth. Add pasta; toss lightly. If desired, add 1 cup frozen peas, thawed, and 1 cup cubed ham.

CREAMY ITALIAN CHICKEN

4 small boneless, skinless chicken breasts, coated lightly with flour

1 tablespoon olive oil

¾ cup chicken broth

4 ounces cream cheese, cubed

2 tablespoons Italian dressing

In large skillet, add chicken to oil and cook for 5 to 6 minutes on each side until done. Remove chicken and reserve drippings. Add broth to drippings and stir. Add cream cheese and Italian dressing. Cook for 3 minutes until cream cheese is melted, stirring constantly with whisk. Return chicken to skillet and coat with sauce. Cook for 2 more minutes. Serve with hot buttered noodles or rice.

CHICKEN AND RICE BAKE

1 (10 ounce) can cream of mushroom soup

1⅓ cups water

¾ cup uncooked instant white rice

¼ teaspoon salt

⅛ teaspoon pepper

4 skinless, boneless chicken breasts

Dash paprika

Mix soup, water, rice, salt, and pepper in shallow baking dish. Place chicken on rice mixture. Sprinkle with paprika. Cover and bake at 375 degrees for 45 minutes or until chicken is no longer pink and rice is done.

BEEF AND BROCCOLI

1 tablespoon butter
¾ pound thin beef strips
1 small sweet onion, sliced
2 cups fresh broccoli florets
½ cup fresh mushrooms, sliced

1 (2 ounce) package brown gravy mix
1 cup water
¼ teaspoon pepper

In large skillet, heat butter over medium-high heat. Add beef strips and onion and sauté for 3 to 4 minutes; add broccoli and mushrooms. In separate bowl, combine gravy mix, water, and pepper. Pour over beef mixture. Stir and bring to a boil. Cover and simmer for 5 to 8 minutes or until broccoli is tender.

BEEF AND NOODLES

½ pound lean ground beef

1 onion, chopped

1 (15 ounce) can chili, no beans

1 (10 ounce) can diced tomatoes with green chilies, drained

1 tablespoon mustard

1 cup cooked elbow macaroni

1 egg, beaten

½ cup shredded cheddar cheese

In large skillet, cook ground beef and onion until beef is browned; drain. Stir in chili, tomatoes, and mustard. Bring to a boil. Reduce heat and simmer for 10 minutes. Remove from heat and add remaining ingredients. Stir and pour into casserole dish. Bake uncovered at 350 degrees for 35 to 40 minutes. Sprinkle with additional cheese if desired.

CHEESY CHICKEN AND BROCCOLI

2 (12 ounce) jars chicken gravy

1 tablespoon lemon juice

2 cups frozen broccoli florets, thawed

2 cups cooked chicken, cubed

1 (10 ounce) package frozen puff pastry shells, baked

½ cup shredded cheddar cheese

Mix gravy, lemon juice, broccoli, and chicken in saucepan. Heat through. Spoon into pastry shells. Sprinkle with cheese. Serve with fresh fruit for a light dinner.

. . . .

CHICKEN POT PIE

1 (10 ounce) can cream of chicken soup

1 (9 ounce) package frozen mixed vegetables, thawed

2 (5 ounce) cans chunk chicken breast

½ cup milk

1 egg

1 cup baking mix

1 teaspoon seasoned salt

Mix soup, vegetables, and chicken in 9-inch pie plate. In separate bowl, mix milk, egg, baking mix, and seasoned salt. Pour over chicken mixture. Bake at 400 degrees for 30 minutes or until golden brown.

TURKEY AND GRAVY SANDWICH

1 (6 ounce) package stuffing
  mix

6 slices bread

1 pound sliced cooked
  turkey breast

1 (12 ounce) jar turkey gravy,
  warmed

Prepare stuffing as directed on package. Place 1 slice bread on each plate. Top with turkey and stuffing. Drizzle with gravy.

. . . .

EASY TURKEY AND BROCCOLI CASSEROLE

2 (10 ounce) packages frozen
  broccoli spears

2 cups diced cooked turkey

1 cup shredded cheddar
  cheese

1 (14½ ounce) can evaporated
  milk

1 can condensed cream of
  chicken soup

1 (3½ ounce) can french-fried
  onions

Preheat oven to 350 degrees. Cook broccoli as directed on package. Layer turkey, broccoli, and cheese in baking dish. Blend evaporated milk and soup. Pour over cheese. Bake for 25 minutes. Top with onions and bake for 5 more minutes.

YUMZETTI

2 pounds ground beef
¼ cup chopped onion
1 can condensed tomato soup
1 (16 ounce) package wide egg
   noodles

1 can condensed cream of
   chicken soup
Shredded cheese (optional)

Brown ground beef; drain. Add onion and tomato soup. Cook noodles according to package directions; drain and add cream of chicken soup. In 9x9-inch pan, layer beef mixture then noodle mixture. Top with cheese if desired. Bake at 350 degrees for 30 minutes.

CREAMY CHICKEN CASSEROLE

¼ cup finely chopped celery

½ cup chopped sweet onion

1 cup fresh mushrooms, sliced

2 tablespoons butter

1 cup sour cream

¾ cup milk

2 (5 ounce) cans chunk chicken breast, drained and flaked

1 cup frozen peas

8 ounces egg noodles, cooked and drained

¼ cup grated Parmesan cheese

In saucepan, cook celery, onion, and mushrooms in butter until tender. Stir in sour cream, milk, chicken, peas, and noodles. Pour into casserole dish. Sprinkle with cheese. Bake for 25 minutes at 350 degrees.

TUNA ALFREDO

1 (16 ounce) package bowtie pasta

1 (10 ounce) package frozen peas and carrots

2 (5 ounce) cans albacore tuna

1 (28 ounce) jar alfredo sauce

1 cup shredded mozzarella cheese

Cook pasta with frozen vegetables according to pasta directions. Drain. Add remaining ingredients and heat through for about 5 minutes on medium heat.

. . . .

CHEESY BAKED SPAGHETTI

8 ounces thin spaghetti

1 pound ground beef

1 jar spaghetti sauce

½ small white onion, finely chopped

1 green pepper, chopped

1 cup shredded mozzarella cheese

Cook spaghetti according to package directions; drain. Brown ground beef; drain. Place spaghetti and ground beef in buttered 9x9-inch baking dish. Cover with spaghetti sauce; stir in onion and green pepper. Top with cheese. Bake at 300 degrees for 25 minutes.

HANDY CONVERSIONS

1 teaspoon = 5 milliliters

1 tablespoon = 15 milliliters

1 fluid ounce = 30 milliliters

1 cup = 250 milliliters

1 pint = 2 cups (or 16 fluid ounces)

1 quart = 4 cups (or 2 pints or 32 fluid ounces)

1 gallon = 16 cups (or 4 quarts)

1 peck = 8 quarts

1 bushel = 4 pecks

1 pound = 454 grams

Fahrenheit	Celsius
250°–300°	121°–149°
300°–325°	149°–163°
325°–350°	163°–177°
375°	191°
400°–425°	204°–218°

POT ROAST WITH CARROTS

1 can condensed cream of
    mushroom soup
1 package dry onion soup mix

1 small package baby carrots
1 (4 pound) boneless chuck
    pot roast

Mix soup, onion soup mix, and carrots in slow cooker. Add
roast; turn to coat. Cover. Cook on low for about 8 hours.

. . . .

SKILLET CHICKEN DINNER

4 boneless, skinless
    chicken breasts
1 (14 ounce) can chicken broth
1 teaspoon garlic salt
¾ cup uncooked white rice

1 (16 ounce) package frozen
    vegetable combination,
    thawed
⅓ cup grated Parmesan
    cheese

Add chicken to skillet coated with cooking spray and cook
until browned. Remove chicken. Add broth, garlic salt, rice, and
vegetables. Heat to a boil. Cover and cook over low heat for 15
minutes. Stir in cheese. Replace chicken. Cover and cook for 10
minutes or until done.

GRANDMA G'S MEAT LOAF

1 onion, chopped

1 cup bread crumbs

1 teaspoon salt

½ teaspoon pepper

½ cup milk

1 egg

1 teaspoon sage

1 pound ground beef

Topping:

½ cup ketchup

1 teaspoon nutmeg

⅔ cup brown sugar

1 teaspoon mustard

Combine all meat loaf ingredients except beef; then add beef and mix well. Form into loaf and put in loaf pan. Topping: In bowl, mix all topping ingredients and spread on meat loaf. Bake at 350 degrees for 1 hour.

SLOW-COOKER ROAST

2 to 3 pounds pot roast

1½ cups water

1 beef bouillon cube

1 package dry onion soup mix

Brown roast in frying pan. Place roast in slow cooker and cover with water. Add beef bouillon and soup mix. Cook on high for 3½ to 4 hours or until roast is falling apart.

. . . .

BROCCOLI CHEESE RICE

1 cup uncooked rice

1 (16 ounce) bag frozen broccoli

1 (10½ ounce) can cream of mushroom soup

1 (10 ounce) jar processed American cheese

Cook rice according to package directions. Steam broccoli in microwave. When both are completely cooked, combine in large bowl. Stir in soup and cheese. Mix thoroughly and serve. Do not add salt.

CHICKEN AND DUMPLINGS

1 whole chicken

1 carrot, sliced

2 cloves garlic

1 teaspoon salt

3 large eggs

5 cups flour

½ teaspoon baking powder

½ teaspoon salt

1 teaspoon pepper

In large pot, cover chicken with water and cook with sliced carrot, garlic, and 1 teaspoon salt. Cook on medium-high heat for 2 hours at a slow boil until chicken flesh falls away from bone. Allow stock to cool completely. In bowl, whisk eggs with 1 cup cold chicken stock from pot. In separate bowl, mix flour, baking powder, ½ teaspoon salt, and pepper. Stir stock-egg mixture into flour mixture to form a dough. Knead dough for 2 minutes and roll out on floured surface to 1 inch thick. Cut out dumplings and pile on floured plate with flour between each layer. Reheat pot of stock and drop in dumplings and deboned chicken pieces. Cook for 5 minutes and serve.

TRY SOMETHING NEW!

*He who was seated on the throne said,
"I am making everything new!"
Then he said, "Write this down, for these
words are trustworthy and true."*

REVELATION 21:5 NIV

BRAIDED STROMBOLI

2 (1 pound) loaves frozen
    bread dough, thawed and
    risen

½ cup spaghetti sauce

½ teaspoon dried oregano

4 ounces sliced pepperoni

¼ pound thinly sliced deli
    ham

¼ pound thinly sliced salami

2 cups shredded mozzarella
    cheese

2 cups shredded cheddar
    cheese

⅓ cup grated Parmesan
    cheese

Preheat oven to 350 degrees. Punch risen dough down. On
lightly floured surface, roll each loaf into 20x8-inch rectangle.
Place 1 rectangle on greased baking sheet. Spread spaghetti
sauce in wide strip down center. Sprinkle with oregano and
top with pepperoni, ham, salami, mozzarella, and cheddar. Fold
long sides of dough up toward filling; set aside. Cut remaining
rectangle into 3 strips. Loosely braid strips; pinch ends to seal.
Place braid on top of cheese; pinch braid to dough to seal.
Sprinkle with Parmesan cheese. Bake for 30 minutes or until
golden brown.

Plan a fun Italian-themed dinner and activities for your family for a weekend evening.

 Use the Braided Stromboli recipe on page 92 and make a pot of spaghetti and meatballs.

 You could also set up a "make-your-own-pizza" table for appetizers or the main course.

 Create a yummy Italian dessert like tiramisu or gelato.

 Cover the table with a red-check tablecloth.

 Play Italian love songs on your iPod or CD player.

 Print out maps of Italy or the Italian flag to use as paper place mats.

 Learn a few Italian phrases as a family.

 Check out a few books from the library about traveling to Italy.

 During dinner, ask this question: "If you were to travel to Italy, what would you do there and why?"

Rent an Italian family-friendly movie like *Lady and the Tramp* to finish off the evening.

Pinterest is a great tool to find theme night and family dinner ideas! Follow my "Family Italian Theme Night" board at http://pinterest.com/marileeparrish/family-italian-theme-night/.

CRAB ST. LAURENT

1 tablespoon butter

1 tablespoon flour

½ cup stock

½ cup cream

½ teaspoon salt

¼ teaspoon pepper

1 cup boiled crabmeat

2 tablespoons grated Parmesan cheese, divided

2 tablespoons white wine vinegar

Buttered toast, cut into fourths

Cayenne pepper to taste

Place saucepan over medium heat with 1 tablespoon butter. When melted, add flour and stir. Slowly add stock and stir until smooth; add cream. When thickened, add salt and pepper, crabmeat, and 1½ tablespoons Parmesan cheese. Simmer for 2 to 3 minutes and add vinegar. Spread mixture over pieces of buttered toast; sprinkle with remaining Parmesan cheese. Broil toast wedges for 3 minutes; sprinkle with cayenne pepper to taste.

HONEY-LIME PORK CHOPS

½ cup lime juice

¼ cup vegetable oil

½ teaspoon cumin

⅛ teaspoon cayenne pepper

2 tablespoons honey

1 tablespoon Dijon mustard

2 garlic cloves, minced

¼ teaspoon salt

½ teaspoon pepper

6 to 8 pork chops

Place all ingredients except pork chops in large resealable plastic bag. Shake ingredients to mix; add pork chops. Seal bag and turn to coat pork chops with mixture. Refrigerate overnight. Drain and discard marinade. Grill chops, covered, over medium heat.

HAM LOAF

1 pound chopped or ground ham

1 pound ground pork

2 eggs

1 cup bread crumbs

1 tablespoon chopped green bell pepper

1 tablespoon chopped onion

¼ teaspoon salt

Flour

Basting Liquid:

2 cups brown sugar

1 teaspoon mustard

⅓ cup crushed pineapple

½ cup water

⅓ cup vinegar

Preheat oven to 350 degrees. Combine meats, eggs, bread crumbs, bell pepper, onion, and salt. Form into loaf and place in greased casserole dish. Sprinkle loaf lightly with flour. In saucepan, combine all basting ingredients and bring to a boil, stirring constantly for 3 minutes, until mixture thickens. Pour basting liquid over loaf and bake for 1 hour, basting often.

CORN BREAD PIE

1 pound ground beef
½ cup chopped onion
1 teaspoon salt
¾ teaspoon pepper
1½ cups water

1 (10½ ounce) can tomato soup
1 (12 ounce) can whole-kernel corn
1 tablespoon chili powder
½ cup chopped green bell pepper

Topping:

1 egg
½ cup milk
1 tablespoon cooking oil
1½ teaspoons baking powder

¾ cup cornmeal
1 tablespoon flour
1 tablespoon sugar

Brown ground beef and onion in frying pan and drain fat. Add remaining ingredients for corn bread pie. Mix well and simmer for 15 minutes. Pour into greased casserole dish. Combine all topping ingredients in frying pan and stir for 2 minutes. Then drop topping mixture on top of casserole mixture. Bake at 350 degrees for 20 minutes.

BEEF AND PEPPER CASSEROLE

2½ cups herb-seasoned
stuffing mix, divided
1 tablespoon butter, melted
1 pound ground beef
1 medium onion, chopped

1 (5 ounce) can diced tomatoes
1 (8 ounce) can corn, drained
2 medium green bell peppers,
quartered

Mix ¼ cup stuffing and butter. Set aside. Cook beef and onion until beef is browned; drain. Stir in tomatoes and corn. Add remaining stuffing. Mix lightly. Place peppers in casserole dish. Spoon beef mixture over peppers. Cover and bake at 400 degrees for 30 minutes. Sprinkle with reserved stuffing mix during last 5 minutes.

TEX-MEX MACARONI DINNER

1 pound lean ground beef

1 red onion, chopped

2 tablespoons taco seasoning

1 cup water

1 (15 ounce) can tomato sauce

8 ounces pasta, cooked and drained

1 (4 ounce) can diced green chilies

1 cup frozen corn

2 cups shredded cheddar cheese

Brown beef and onion. Drain. Add taco seasoning, water, and tomato sauce. Bring to a boil and simmer for 10 minutes. Stir in cooked macaroni, chilies, and corn. Pour into greased 9x13-inch baking dish. Top with cheddar cheese. Bake at 350 degrees for 25 minutes.

CHEESY TORTELLINI AND PEAS

1 (10 ounce) package frozen
tortellini

2 cups frozen peas

1 (28 ounce) jar alfredo sauce

2 cups shredded mozzarella
cheese

Grated Parmesan cheese
(optional)

Cook tortellini and peas in same pot according to pasta directions. Add alfredo sauce and cheese. Heat for 3 to 5 minutes on medium heat. Top with grated Parmesan cheese, if desired.

CREAMY CHICKEN AND ASPARAGUS

8 sprigs fresh asparagus, cut in half

2 tablespoons butter

1 (28 ounce) jar alfredo sauce

2 cups cooked chicken, cubed

2 cups shredded mozzarella cheese

1 (16 ounce) package penne pasta, cooked and drained

Cook asparagus in butter and add alfredo sauce. Cook on low for 3 to 5 minutes. Add remaining ingredients and cook for 3 to 4 minutes until cheese is almost melted.

· ·

CHICKEN SPAGHETTI

1 whole chicken, cooked

1 cup diced celery

1 cup diced onion

2 cups chicken broth

1 (10½ ounce) can cream of mushroom soup

1 pound Velveeta cheese, cubed

16 ounces spaghetti, cooked and drained

1 small jar pimientos

Debone cooked chicken. In large saucepan, heat celery and onion in chicken broth on medium-high heat for 15 minutes. Reduce heat to medium and stir in soup and cheese until melted. Combine chicken, cooked spaghetti, and pimientos in large casserole dish; pour hot soup mixture over top. Mix well and bake at 350 degrees for 20 to 30 minutes or until hot and bubbly.

 MORE CONVERSATION STARTERS

Ask these questions during a family dinner:

 What do you want to be doing five years from now?

 What do you think you'll look like in five years? Ten years?

 Where do you think you'll live in twenty years?

What would you do with one million dollars?

 If our house ever caught on fire and you could only grab one thing, what would it be and why? (Make sure to review your emergency plan together and reassure young children that the likelihood of this ever happening is very small! But do go over precautions to help children feel prepared instead of scared!)

BBQ CHICKEN PIZZA

1 cup barbecue sauce

1 large store-bought pizza crust

1 cup chopped cooked chicken

1 small red onion, sliced

2 cups shredded cheddar cheese

Spread barbecue sauce on crust. Arrange remaining ingredients on crust. Bake as directed on crust package.

. . . .

VEGETABLE PIZZA

1 cup fresh mushrooms, sliced

1 small onion, sliced

1 tablespoon butter

1 (10 ounce) jar prepared basil pesto

1 large store-bought pizza crust

1 large tomato, diced

Sauté mushrooms and onions in butter. Spread pesto on crust. Arrange remaining ingredients on crust, including mushrooms and onions. Bake as directed on crust package.

GLAZED HAM LOAF DINNER

1 pound ground pork

1 pound ground ham

10 butter crackers, crushed

2 eggs

1¼ cups milk

1 teaspoon mustard

4 red potatoes, pierced with fork

Sauce:

⅓ cup crushed pineapple

½ cup brown sugar

½ teaspoon mustard

¼ cup water

Mix pork, ham, crumbs, eggs, milk, and mustard. Form into loaf and place in roasting pan. Surround with potatoes. Combine sauce ingredients and pour over loaf. Bake at 350 degrees for 1½ hours.

SPAGHETTI SKILLETINI

1 (28 ounce) jar spaghetti sauce

2 cups water

1 (12 ounce) package spaghetti, broken in half

1 green bell pepper, diced

½ cup shredded mozzarella cheese

½ cup grated Parmesan cheese

In large skillet, combine spaghetti sauce and water. Bring to a boil over medium-high heat. Add spaghetti and stir well, making sure spaghetti is completely covered in sauce. Bring to a boil again. Cover and reduce heat to low. Simmer for 20 minutes, stirring frequently. Add bell pepper and cook until spaghetti is almost tender. Top with cheeses and serve immediately.

PEPPER STEAK STIR-FRY

½ cup steak sauce

¼ cup soy sauce

1 to 1½ tablespoons cornstarch

1 pound beef top round steak, sliced thin

1 tablespoon oil

1 green bell pepper, cut into strips

1 small sweet onion, sliced

¾ cup beef broth

Mix steak sauce, soy sauce, and cornstarch. Coat meat and drain, reserving sauce. Cook and stir meat in hot oil in large skillet for 3 minutes. Add pepper and onion; cook for 1 minute. Add beef broth and reserved sauce; bring to a boil. Reduce heat; simmer for 1 minute. Serve with rice.

BBQ CHICKEN FAJITAS

1 to 1½ cups instant white rice, uncooked

1 to 1½ cups hot water

1 tablespoon taco seasoning mix

4 small boneless, skinless chicken breasts

4 tablespoons prepared barbecue sauce

1 each green and red bell pepper, cut into strips

½ cup chunky salsa

½ cup Mexican-style finely shredded cheese

Preheat oven to 400 degrees. Combine rice, water, and taco seasoning and spoon onto greased heavy-duty foil or foil packet. Top with remaining ingredients, spreading barbecue sauce on top of chicken. Seal each packet well, allowing room for heat to circulate. Bake for 35 minutes or until chicken is no longer pink in the center. Let stand for 5 minutes before serving. Serve with warm tortillas.

PINEAPPLE PORK CHOPS

Salt and pepper to taste
6 to 8 pork chops
Cooking oil

1 (16 ounce) can crushed
pineapple, undrained
1 cup minute rice, uncooked

Salt and pepper pork chops. Cover bottom of frying pan with cooking oil. Brown chops on each side over medium heat. Pour crushed pineapple with juice over pork chops. Reduce heat to low, cover, and cook for 35 minutes. Slide chops to one side of frying pan and pour rice into remaining pineapple and juice. Add water if needed. Replace lid and cook until pork chops test done.

FIESTA CHICKEN AND RICE BAKE

1 (10 ounce) can cream of chicken soup

1 cup salsa

½ cup water

1 cup whole-kernel corn

¾ cup long-grain white rice, uncooked

4 boneless chicken breast halves

Dash paprika

½ cup shredded cheddar cheese

½ cup finely chopped red bell pepper

Mix soup, salsa, water, corn, and rice in shallow baking dish. Top with chicken and sprinkle with paprika. Cover and bake at 375 degrees for 45 minutes or until done. Sprinkle with cheese and bell pepper.

• •

MEXICAN-STYLE STUFFED PEPPERS

3 cups cooked white rice

1 cup whole-kernel corn

½ cup chopped green onions

1¾ cups salsa, divided

1½ cups cheddar cheese, divided

4 green and 4 red bell peppers, halved and seeded

Combine rice, corn, green onions, ¾ cup salsa, and 1 cup cheese in large bowl. Fill each pepper with about ½ cup rice mixture. Place peppers in ungreased 9x13-inch baking dish; top with remaining salsa and cheese. Bake at 350 degrees for 20 to 25 minutes.

MEAT PIE

1 pound ground beef, browned
and drained

¼ cup chopped onion

1 (10 ounce) package frozen
peas and carrots, thawed

1 cup chopped cooked
potatoes

2 cups shredded cheddar
cheese

2 tablespoons flour

½ teaspoon salt

2 tablespoons butter, melted

1 cup water

1 (8 ounce) tube refrigerated
crescent rolls

Place beef, vegetables, and cheese in 9x13-inch baking dish.
In saucepan, add flour and salt to butter; whisk and cook for
2 minutes. Add water and bring to a boil, stirring constantly.
Simmer on low for 3 minutes. Pour over meat. Unroll dough
and place over meat. Press seams together. Bake at 375 degrees
for 25 minutes.

CHEESE AND CHICKEN ENCHILADAS

1 small onion, chopped
1 tablespoon butter
1½ cups shredded cooked
chicken breast
4 ounces cream cheese

¾ cup shredded cheddar
cheese, divided
1 (16 ounce) jar salsa, divided
8 flour tortillas

Sauté onion in butter. Add chicken, cream cheese, ½ cup cheddar, and ¾ cup salsa. Heat and stir until cheeses are melted. Spoon ⅓ cup of mixture in each tortilla. Roll up and place in lightly greased 9x13-inch baking dish. Spread remaining salsa over tortillas and top with remaining cheese. Cover and bake for 15 to 20 minutes at 350 degrees.

CHICKEN NACHO SALAD

1 tablespoon vegetable oil

1 pound boneless, skinless chicken breasts, cut into strips

1 (16 ounce) can whole-kernel corn, drained

1 (15 ounce) can tomato sauce

1 (4 ounce) can diced green chilies

1 teaspoon chili powder

1 teaspoon onion powder

Tortilla chips

3 cups shredded lettuce

1 cup shredded cheddar cheese

In large skillet, heat oil over medium heat. Add chicken and cook for 5 minutes. Stir in corn, tomato sauce, chilies, chili powder, and onion powder; heat to a boil. Reduce heat to medium and cook for 10 minutes, stirring occasionally. Layer tortilla chips and lettuce together in individual bowls. Spoon chicken mixture onto lettuce and top with cheese.

PORK AND FENNEL RAGOUT

1 cup finely chopped onion

1 cup finely chopped fennel

2 garlic cloves, minced

1 tablespoon fennel seeds

2 teaspoons sugar

1 teaspoon oregano

½ teaspoon salt

½ teaspoon crushed red pepper flakes

¼ teaspoon black pepper

¼ teaspoon ground red pepper

8 ounces lean ground pork

½ cup fat-free, low-sodium chicken broth

2 cups chopped tomato

4 cups hot cooked rigatoni

Heat large skillet coated with cooking spray over medium-high heat. Add onion, fennel, and garlic; cook for 5 minutes. Add fennel seeds, sugar, oregano, salt, red pepper flakes, black pepper, ground red pepper, and pork, stirring to combine. Sauté for 3 minutes. Add broth and tomato; bring to a boil. Reduce heat and simmer for 15 minutes, stirring occasionally. Serve over hot rigatoni.

FRENCH SAUSAGE CASSOULET

½ cup chopped carrots

½ cup chopped red onion

1 teaspoon finely chopped
fresh garlic

2 tablespoons butter

2 (15 ounce) cans great
northern beans, rinsed and
drained

¼ pound kielbasa, cut into
¼-inch slices

1 (8 ounce) can tomato sauce

½ teaspoon thyme

¼ cup butter cracker crumbs

3 tablespoons chopped fresh
parsley

Sauté carrots, onion, and garlic with butter in skillet. Combine
onion mixture, beans, kielbasa, tomato sauce, and thyme in
greased casserole dish. Sprinkle with cracker crumbs. Cover
and bake for 35 to 45 minutes at 350 degrees. Sprinkle with
parsley.

FETA CHICKEN AND RICE

4 to 5 boneless, skinless
   chicken breasts

2 tablespoons lemon juice,
   divided

½ teaspoon salt

¼ teaspoon pepper

1 (4 ounce) package crumbled
   feta cheese

¼ cup diced fresh tomatoes

¼ cup finely chopped green
   bell pepper

¼ cup chopped fresh parsley

Arrange chicken in 9x13-inch baking dish. Sprinkle with 1
tablespoon lemon juice. Season with salt and pepper. Top with
feta cheese and sprinkle remaining lemon juice on top. Bake
at 350 degrees for 35 to 40 minutes or until chicken is cooked
through. Sprinkle with tomatoes, bell pepper, and parsley. Serve
with hot cooked rice.

Don't worry about anything; instead, pray about everything. Tell God what you need, and thank him for all he has done. Then you will experience God's peace, which exceeds anything we can understand. His peace will guard your hearts and minds as you live in Christ Jesus.

PHILIPPIANS 4:6–7 NLT

· · · · ·

Heavenly Father, as we gather for dinner as a family this evening, please bless our time together. Help us to trust You with all of our hearts. Stressful feelings mean that we aren't fully allowing You to carry our burdens. Please give us Your peace to guard our hearts and minds. Amen.

HAM STEAKS

4 to 6 ham slices, about ½ inch thick

1¼ cups cranberry juice

½ cup light brown sugar

½ cup raisins

½ cup orange juice

2 tablespoons cornstarch

Dash ground cloves

Arrange ham slices evenly in 9x13-inch baking dish. In saucepan, combine remaining ingredients. Cook and stir over medium heat until thick and bubbly. Pour over ham slices. Bake uncovered at 350 degrees for 30 to 40 minutes.

. . . .

FESTIVAL FISH DINNER

2 pounds white fish fillets

½ cup french dressing

1½ cups crushed butter crackers

2 tablespoons butter, melted

Dash paprika

Skin fillets and cut into equal portions. Dip fish into dressing and roll in cracker crumbs. Place on greased cookie sheet. Drizzle butter over fish. Sprinkle with paprika. Bake at 500 degrees for 10 to 12 minutes or until fish flakes easily. Serve with french fries and coleslaw.

SPINACH RAVIOLI

2 cups water

1 (10 ounce) package frozen creamed spinach

1 (24 ounce) package frozen cheese ravioli

1 (16 ounce) jar alfredo sauce

½ cup shredded Parmesan cheese

Boil water in large pot. Add spinach pouch and return to boil. Cook for 3 minutes. Add ravioli; return to boil. Reduce heat and simmer for 5 minutes until ravioli float. Drain and remove spinach. Place spinach in large skillet. Add alfredo sauce and mix gently. Heat for 5 minutes until mixture just begins to bubble, stirring frequently. Add ravioli and stir. Sprinkle with cheese.

• •

ITALIAN SHRIMP AND BROCCOLI

1 (15 ounce) can diced garlic and herb tomatoes, undrained

1 tablespoon ketchup

2 cups frozen broccoli, thawed

½ pound cooked shrimp

Heat tomatoes, ketchup, and broccoli over medium-high heat for 3 to 5 minutes. Stir in cooked shrimp. Simmer until hot and serve over rice.

TOMATO TORTELLINI DINNER

1 (20 ounce) package frozen cheese tortellini

1 tablespoon butter

1 small onion, chopped

1 green bell pepper, chopped

1 (15 ounce) can diced tomatoes

1 tablespoon half-and-half

1 (24 ounce) jar spaghetti sauce

Cook frozen tortellini according to package directions. Meanwhile, melt butter in large saucepan. Sauté onion and green pepper. Add tomatoes, half-and-half, and spaghetti sauce. Heat for 3 to 5 minutes. Drain cooked tortellini and add to sauce. Mix gently. Top with cheese if desired.

GRILLED KEBABS

1 cup ketchup

1 teaspoon salt

2 tablespoons steak sauce

2 tablespoons Worcestershire sauce

1 tablespoon sugar

2 tablespoons apple cider vinegar

2 tablespoons olive oil

¼ cup water

Steak, cut into cubes

Boneless, skinless chicken, cut into cubes

Sliced vegetables

In saucepan, mix all ingredients except meat and vegetables. Bring to a boil. Pour over meat. Refrigerate for 2 hours or overnight. Alternate on skewer with your favorite vegetables. Grill over medium heat, basting with leftover marinade.

PEPPER AND ZUCCHINI STIR-FRY

¼ cup olive oil

2 zucchini, sliced

½ cup chopped cooked
  chicken

1 to 2 cloves fresh garlic

1 teaspoon salt

¼ teaspoon pepper

6 bell peppers of multi colors,
  washed and cut into strips

1 cup shredded mozzarella
  cheese

Heat oil and sauté zucchini and chicken for 4 to 5 minutes until lightly browned. Stir in garlic, salt, and pepper and cook for 1 minute. Add bell peppers and sauté. Remove from heat and add cheese. Serve with white rice.

A NEW CREATION

Allow your kids to get creative and concoct a new recipe of their own. Try adapting a cookie recipe to include a favorite kind of candy, or a casserole dish with a different kind of cheese or vegetable. You can get as adventurous as you want, but be prepared for a few failures before you get an edible result.

• • • • •

Therefore, if anyone is in Christ, the new creation has come: The old has gone, the new is here!

2 CORINTHIANS 5:17 NIV

CRANBERRY-GLAZED HAM DINNER

2 oranges, sliced

5-pound fully cooked ham

¼ cup whole cloves

4 small red potatoes, pierced
  with fork

½ cup brown sugar

2 tablespoons honey

½ cup cranberry juice cocktail

1 tablespoon mustard

¼ teaspoon nutmeg

Arrange orange slices on ham in roasting pan. Press cloves into ham surface. Place potatoes around ham. Bake at 325 degrees for 90 minutes. Mix remaining ingredients together. During last 40 minutes, brush ham with mixture.

ONE-POT TURKEY DINNER

1-pound turkey tenderloin

1 teaspoon salt

⅓ cup whole cranberries

½ cup orange juice

Dash pepper

⅓ cup walnuts, chopped

1 small onion, sliced

2 medium sweet potatoes, sliced

2 cups broccoli florets

Place turkey into roasting pan and lightly sprinkle with salt. Chop cranberries, orange juice, pepper, and walnuts in blender until just mixed. Using spoon, drop half of cranberry mix on turkey. Layer onions and sweet potato slices around turkey. Cover with remaining cranberry mix. Top with broccoli. Cover and bake at 450 degrees for 40 minutes or until done.

FIESTA FISH

1 pound frozen haddock or cod fillets, thawed

1 medium zucchini, sliced

1 medium yellow squash, sliced

1¼ cups chunky salsa, divided

½ cup finely shredded mozzarella cheese

Cut fish into 4 pieces. Mix zucchini, squash, and 1 cup salsa in 9-inch square baking dish. Top with fish. Spoon 1 tablespoon remaining salsa over each piece of fish. Bake at 400 degrees for 15 minutes. Sprinkle each piece of fish with cheese. Bake an additional 8 to 12 minutes or until cheese is melted and fish is done.

. . . .

QUICK GUMBO

½ pound sliced smoked sausage, browned

2 (14 ounce) cans diced tomatoes, undrained

2 tablespoons Cajun seasoning

1 (10 ounce) package mixed vegetables, thawed

½ pound cooked shrimp

Add all ingredients to skillet except shrimp. Cook for 4 to 5 minutes. Stir in shrimp. Heat for 3 minutes just until shrimp are hot. Serve with rice.

SALMON CAKES

½ cup fine bread crumbs

1 stalk celery, very finely chopped

2 tablespoons mayonnaise

2 tablespoons finely diced onion

1 tablespoon parsley flakes

1 teaspoon lemon pepper seasoning

1 teaspoon baking powder

1 egg, beaten

1 (16 ounce) can pink salmon, drained and deboned

Place all ingredients except salmon in large bowl and mix well. Add salmon and mix gently but thoroughly. Shape into 4 patties. Place patties on lightly greased broiler pan and broil for 4 minutes on each side 8 inches from source of heat. Serve with baby spinach.

PENNE AND SHRIMP DINNER

1 pound raw shrimp, peeled, deveined

1 teaspoon kosher salt

¼ teaspoon pepper

3 tablespoons olive oil

2 garlic cloves, minced

6 plum tomatoes, sliced thin

¼ cup chopped fresh cilantro, divided

3 tablespoons lime juice

6 ounces baby spinach leaves

12 ounces multigrain penne pasta, cooked

3 tablespoons water

Sprinkle shrimp with salt and pepper. Add oil, shrimp, and garlic to skillet and sauté for 2 minutes. Add tomatoes, half of cilantro, and lime juice. Sauté for 3 minutes or until shrimp is no longer transparent. Add spinach and pasta. Add water and stir. Top with remaining cilantro and serve.

SWEET AND SPICY PORK DINNER

1-pound pork tenderloin

¼ cup french dressing, divided

½ teaspoon chili powder

¼ teaspoon dry mustard

¼ teaspoon paprika

¼ teaspoon thyme

1 tablespoon honey

Brush meat with 2 tablespoons french dressing. Mix dry ingredients and rub onto meat. Place in baking pan. Mix remaining 2 tablespoons dressing with honey and set aside. Bake at 425 degrees for 15 minutes. Brush with dressing mixture. Bake an additional 10 minutes or until cooked through. Remove meat from oven and cover with foil. Let stand for 5 minutes before slicing. Serve with hot cooked rice.

ONE-DISH PORK DINNER

½ cup packed brown sugar

2 tablespoons butter, cut up

1 teaspoon ground cinnamon

6 boneless pork loin chops

1 small acorn squash, seeded and cut into rings

1 large unpeeled red apple, cored and sliced

Mix brown sugar, butter, and cinnamon until crumbly; set aside. Place pork in 9x13-inch baking dish. Arrange squash and apples around pork. Sprinkle with brown sugar mixture. Bake at 350 degrees for 40 to 45 minutes or until squash is tender and pork is done.

CRAB PRIMAVERA

1½ cups of your favorite frozen vegetables

¼ cup water

1⅓ cups milk

¾ pound crabmeat

2 tablespoons butter

1 teaspoon garlic powder

¾ teaspoon dried basil

1½ cups instant white rice, uncooked

1 cup shredded mozzarella cheese

Bring vegetables and water to a boil in medium saucepan, stirring occasionally. Reduce heat. Cover and simmer for 3 minutes. Add milk, crabmeat, butter, garlic powder, and basil. Bring to a full boil. Stir in rice and cover. Remove from heat. Let stand for 5 minutes. Fluff with fork and top with cheese.

Work willingly at whatever you do, as though you were working for the Lord rather than for people. Remember that the Lord will give you an inheritance as your reward, and that the Master you are serving is Christ.

• • • • •

Heavenly Father, as I prepare dinner for my family tonight, help me to do so willingly, knowing that I'm pleasing You with a right heart as I cook. Thank You for my kitchen and our home. Thank You for the blessing of my family. Amen.

APRICOT CHICKEN DINNER

5 to 6 boneless, skinless chicken breasts

4 red potatoes, pierced with fork

1 cup baby carrots

1 (16 ounce) bottle Russian dressing

1 cup mayonnaise

1 cup apricot jam

2 envelopes onion soup mix

Place chicken in baking pan. Surround chicken with potatoes and carrots. Mix remaining ingredients and pour over chicken and vegetables. Bake at 350 degrees for 1 hour or until chicken is done and veggies are tender.

BAYOU CASSEROLE

½ cup chopped green pepper

1 cup chopped celery

½ cup chopped onion

2 tablespoons butter

2 pounds fresh cooked shrimp

1 pound fresh cooked scallops

1 cup cooked rice

1 small jar pimientos, drained and chopped

¾ cup half-and-half

1 can cream of mushroom soup

1 cup mayonnaise

1 tablespoon Worcestershire sauce

Dash white pepper

Sauté green pepper, celery, and onion in butter. Toss all ingredients together and put in buttered baking dish. Bake uncovered at 375 degrees for 35 minutes or until heated through.

SOUPS, VEGGIES, AND APPETIZERS

Only the pure in heart can make a good soup.

LUDWIG VAN BEETHOVEN

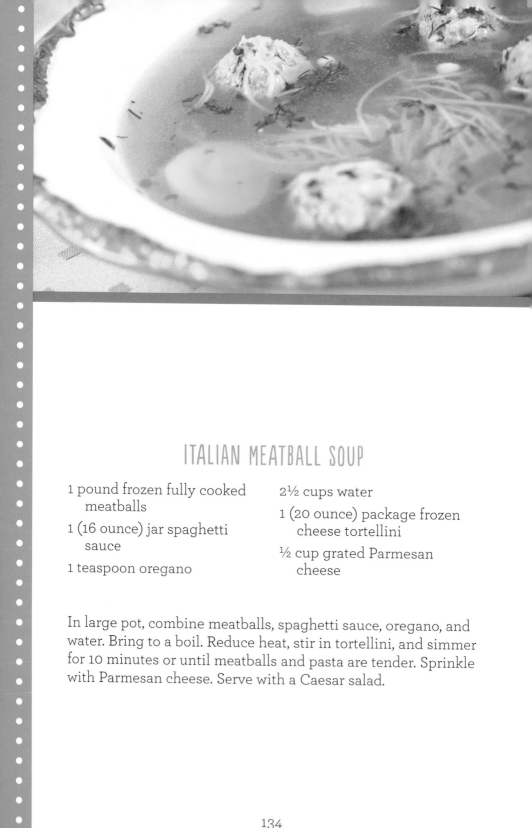

ITALIAN MEATBALL SOUP

1 pound frozen fully cooked
    meatballs

1 (16 ounce) jar spaghetti
    sauce

1 teaspoon oregano

2½ cups water

1 (20 ounce) package frozen
    cheese tortellini

½ cup grated Parmesan
    cheese

In large pot, combine meatballs, spaghetti sauce, oregano, and water. Bring to a boil. Reduce heat, stir in tortellini, and simmer for 10 minutes or until meatballs and pasta are tender. Sprinkle with Parmesan cheese. Serve with a Caesar salad.

BROCCOLI LUNCH SALAD

1 cup mayonnaise

2 tablespoons cider vinegar

2 tablespoons sugar

2 bunches raw broccoli, chopped

1 cup sunflower seeds

½ cup raisins

6 slices cooked bacon, crumbled

½ cup chopped cooked chicken breast

Mix together mayo, vinegar, and sugar. Blend well. Put chopped broccoli in large bowl. Add dressing and remaining ingredients. Mix well.

. . . .

CHICKEN FETA SALAD

4 cups fresh broccoli florets

1 small cucumber, sliced

½ cup chopped red onion

1 green bell pepper, chopped

½ cup crumbled feta cheese

1 (4 ounce) can sliced black olives, drained

½ cup chopped cooked chicken

Combine all ingredients and toss with your favorite dressing.

SHRIMP SALAD

4 cups fresh broccoli florets
1 cup cooked shrimp
1 green onion, chopped

¼ cup chopped celery
1 red bell pepper, chopped

Dressing:
1 cup real mayonnaise
¼ cup lemon juice

¼ cup sugar
1 teaspoon dill

Mix dressing ingredients and toss with remaining ingredients. Refrigerate for 2 to 3 hours before serving.

· ·

CHICKEN PASTA SALAD

6 ounces multicolor pasta, cooked, drained, and rinsed
1 stalk celery, chopped
1 carrot, chopped
1 green onion, chopped
6 to 8 cherry tomatoes, cut in half

¼ cup sliced black olives
2 baked chicken breasts, chopped
¼ cup grated Parmesan cheese
½ cup Italian dressing

Mix all ingredients together and serve.

136

EGG SALAD

5 to 6 hard-boiled eggs, chopped

¼ cup chopped celery

¼ cup chopped onion

¼ cup real mayonnaise

1 tablespoon mustard

1 teaspoon sugar

1 teaspoon salt

½ teaspoon pepper

Mix all ingredients together and serve on lettuce or toast.

. . . .

GRAPE CHICKEN SALAD

2 (5 ounce) cans chicken breast, drained

¼ cup mayonnaise

¼ cup chopped sweet onion

6 to 8 red seedless grapes, cut in half

¼ cup chopped walnuts

1 teaspoon seasoned salt

Mix all ingredients together and serve on lettuce or toast.

ANGELA'S SPINACH SALAD

1 pound fresh baby spinach

6 slices bacon, cooked and crumbled

½ pound fresh mushrooms, sliced

1 sweet onion, sliced

Dressing:

1 cup olive oil

¼ cup sugar

⅓ cup ketchup

¼ cup apple cider vinegar

½ teaspoon salt

2 teaspoons Worcestershire sauce

Mix dressing ingredients and refrigerate. Combine salad ingredients and top with dressing. Top with toasted almonds, strawberries, and/or mandarin oranges if desired. Serve immediately.

WHITE CHICKEN CHILI SOUP

1 tablespoon vegetable oil

1 (12½ ounce) can chunk chicken breast (in water)

1 package white chicken chili seasoning mix

1 cup water

1 (15 ounce) can white beans, undrained

1 (14½ ounce) can stewed tomatoes

1 small can diced tomatoes

1 (8¾ ounce) can southwestern-style corn

Heat oil in large skillet on medium-high heat. Add chicken and stir for 5 minutes or until brown. Stir in seasoning mix, water, beans, tomatoes, and corn. Bring to a boil. Reduce heat to low; cover and simmer for 10 minutes.

GRAPE SALAD

½ cup sugar

1 cup cream cheese

1 cup sour cream

2 pounds red grapes

2 pounds green grapes

1 cup packed brown sugar

1 cup chopped pecans

Cream together sugar, cream cheese, and sour cream. In large serving bowl, stir creamed mixture into grapes. Combine brown sugar and pecans and sprinkle on grape mixture. Refrigerate for 1 hour before serving.

HOT TACO SOUP

2 pounds ground beef

1 large onion, chopped

1 (15 ounce) can pinto beans

1 can whole-kernel corn, drained

1 can Mexican-style stewed tomatoes

1 can diced tomatoes

1 package taco seasoning mix

1 package ranch dressing mix

2½ cups water

Brown ground beef and onion in large pot; drain fat. Add remaining ingredients and simmer for 1½ hours.

STEAK SOUP

1½ pounds ground chuck

½ cup chopped onion

2 tablespoons butter or margarine

1 cup flour

6 cups water

1 tablespoon browning sauce (such as Kitchen Bouquet or Gravy Master)

3 beef bouillon cubes

2 (10 ounce) packages frozen mixed vegetables

1 stalk celery, chopped

1 (11 ounce) can tomatoes

In large pot, brown meat and onion in butter. Stir in flour and gradually add water, browning sauce, and bouillon. Add mixed vegetables, celery, and tomatoes. Cook slowly on low heat on stove for 2½ hours, stirring often.

SALTY SOUP TIP

If your soup has been oversalted, cut up a raw potato or two and drop into the pot.

The potato will absorb some of the salt.

• • • • •

A bowl of vegetables with someone you love
is better than steak with someone you hate.

PROVERBS 15:17 NLT

CRUNCHY CABBAGE SALAD

1 head Napa cabbage, finely sliced

5 green onions, thinly sliced

Dressing:

1 cup sugar

½ cup cider vinegar

2 tablespoons soy sauce

1 package ramen noodles seasoning (chicken)

Topping:

⅓ cup butter

½ cup sliced almonds

2 tablespoons sesame seeds

Noodles from ramen package, crushed

In large bowl combine Napa cabbage and green onions. Refrigerate until ready for use. Dressing: Mix all ingredients in jar and set aside, but periodically shake jar until sugar is completely dissolved. Topping: Melt butter in skillet. Add almonds, sesame seeds, and crushed noodles. Fry until golden brown, stirring continually. Before serving, add topping to cabbage-onion mixture, and pour dressing over all. Mix well.

NACHO TACO SALAD

1 (2 ounce) package taco
  seasoning

1 pound ground beef, browned

1 (16 ounce) bottle french
  dressing

1 medium-sized head iceberg
  lettuce, chopped

2 large tomatoes, chopped

1 large green bell pepper,
  chopped

4 cups cheesy nacho chips,
  crushed

Mix taco seasoning with beef according to package directions.
Let cool. Mix all ingredients together and serve immediately.
Top with sour cream and sliced black olives.

. . . .

FRIED EGGPLANT

1 eggplant

1 quart water

1 tablespoon salt

1 egg

Bread crumbs

Butter or oil

Peel eggplant and cut into thin slices; lay slices in bowl. Mix
water with salt; pour over eggplant. Place a small plate on top
of slices to keep them under salt water. Soak in water for at
least 3 hours. When ready to cook, remove eggplant slices from
bowl and dry with paper towel. Beat egg in bowl. Dip eggplant
slices in egg and then in bread crumbs. In skillet, fry eggplant
in butter or oil.

TERIYAKI MEATBALLS

Meatballs:

2 eggs

2 pounds ground round steak

½ cup cornflake crumbs

½ cup milk

2 tablespoons grated onion

1 teaspoon salt

¼ teaspoon pepper

Mix all meatball ingredients and shape into meatballs about 1½ inches in diameter. Bake at 300 degrees for 45 minutes, turning every 15 minutes.

Sauce:

1 cup soy sauce

2 teaspoons ginger juice or 1 teaspoon powdered ginger

2 cloves garlic, minced

½ cup water

1 teaspoon sugar

Combine all sauce ingredients and pour over meatballs, cooking until heated through.

CHEESE PUFFS

¾ cup margarine or butter

1 (3 ounce) package cream
  cheese

8 ounces shredded sharp
  cheddar cheese

Tabasco sauce

Garlic salt

Worcestershire sauce

2 egg whites, beaten until stiff

1 loaf white bread, frozen

Melt margarine and cheeses. Add seasonings. Fold in beaten
egg whites. Cut crusts off frozen loaf. Cut bread in cubes and
dip each cube in cheese mixture. Place on greased baking sheet
and refrigerate overnight. Bake at 350 degrees for 15 minutes.

CHEESY CREAM CORN

1 (8 ounce) package shredded cheddar cheese

2 (8 ounce) packages cream cheese

3 pounds frozen corn

¼ cup butter or margarine

3 tablespoons milk

1 small can green chilies

3 tablespoons water

Mix all ingredients in slow cooker. Cook on low for 4 hours, until bubbly.

. . . .

SUCCOTASH

1 cup sweet corn

2 cups string beans, cut into 2-inch pieces

1 cup lima beans

Salt and pepper to taste

1 tablespoon butter

⅛ cup brown-rice flour

Place corn, string beans, and lima beans in large saucepan. Add enough water to cover vegetables, and put on medium-high heat to boil. Add salt and pepper to taste. When beans are tender, add butter and a little more salt and pepper. Thicken mixture with brown-rice flour.

PASTA VEGGIE SOUP

2 teaspoons olive oil
6 cloves garlic, minced
1½ cups shredded carrots
1 cup chopped onion
1 cup thinly sliced celery

4 cups chicken broth
4 cups water
1½ cups uncooked ditalini pasta
¼ cup grated Parmesan cheese

In 6-quart dutch oven, heat oil over medium heat. Add garlic and stir for 15 seconds. Add carrots, onion, and celery and cook for 5 minutes until tender, stirring constantly. Add chicken broth and water and bring to a boil. Add pasta and cook for 7 to 10 minutes until pasta is tender. Top each serving with Parmesan cheese.

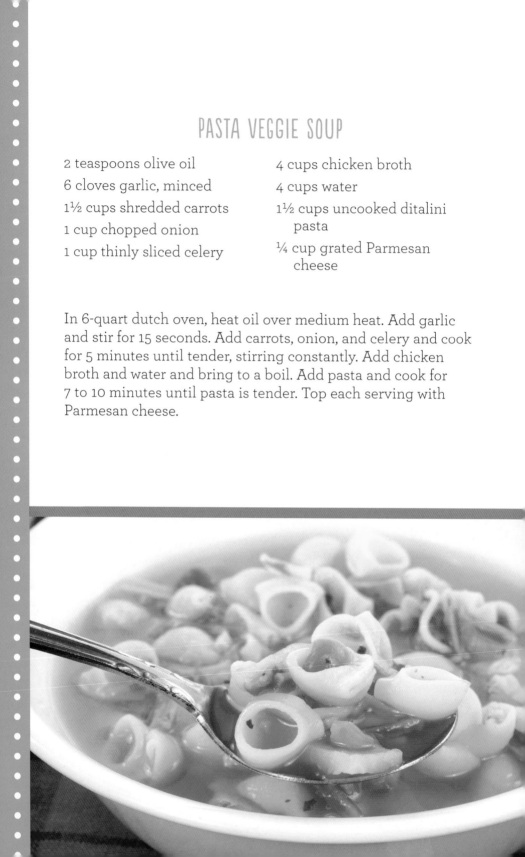

CORN CHIP SALAD

1 can ranch-style beans

1 small head lettuce

2 tomatoes

1 small onion

½ pound shredded cheddar cheese

½ bottle Catalina salad dressing

1 pound corn chips, crushed

Drain and rinse beans. Chop lettuce, tomatoes, and onion. In large bowl, toss all ingredients except salad dressing and corn chips together. Chill in refrigerator for at least 15 minutes. Pour salad dressing over salad and add crushed corn chips immediately before serving.

ZUCCHINI BAKE

3 cups chopped zucchini
¾ cup chopped onion
1½ cups biscuit mix

Salt and pepper to taste
½ cup vegetable oil
6 eggs

Preheat oven to 350 degrees. Grease 9x13-inch baking pan. In large bowl, mix all ingredients. Spread mixture into pan. Bake for 40 minutes, until golden brown. Cut into 2-inch squares and serve at room temperature.

. . . .

APPLE AND NUT SALAD

4 tablespoons vinegar
2 eggs
1 heaping teaspoon butter
1 teaspoon mustard
Dash salt

¼ teaspoon red and white pepper
1 teaspoon sugar
¾ cup whipped topping
½ cup chopped apples
½ cup chopped walnuts

In saucepan, let vinegar come to a boil; stir in eggs until mixture thickens. Cool. Stir in butter, mustard, salt, pepper, and sugar. Add whipped topping before serving and fold in apples and walnuts.

SAUSAGE LENTIL STEW

½ pound bulk Italian sausage

1 large onion, finely chopped

1 small green bell pepper, finely chopped

1 small carrot, grated or finely chopped

1 large garlic clove, minced

1 bay leaf

2 (14½ ounce) cans chicken broth

1 (14½ ounce) can coarsely chopped tomatoes, with liquid

1 cup water

¾ cup dry lentils

Brown and drain sausage. Combine all ingredients in large saucepan and simmer for 1 hour. Remove bay leaf and serve.

TORTILLA ROLLS

4 green onions
1 jalapeño pepper
½ can black olives

1 tablespoon mayonnaise
1 (8 ounce) package cream cheese
1 package soft tortillas

Chop green onions, jalapeño, and olives and place in bowl. Add mayonnaise and cream cheese; blend well. Spread thin layer on each tortilla. Roll up. Refrigerate for 3 minutes. Cut rolls into ½-inch slices and place slices on serving plate.

AVOCADO TREAT

Avocado
Lemon juice
Chili powder
Salt
Lemon pepper

Garlic salt
Tabasco sauce
Mayonnaise
Saltine crackers

Peel avocado and cut into thin slices. Fan slices out on small plate. Squeeze lemon juice over arrangement; then sprinkle all dry spices onto avocado slices to taste. Drop on Tabasco to taste. Spread mayonnaise on crackers and top with prepped avocado.

MINI PIZZA BAGELS

2 bags mini bagels
1 (8 ounce) can pizza sauce
2 teaspoons oregano
Sliced mushrooms

Sliced pepperoni
Minced onions
Minced green bell peppers
Shredded mozzarella cheese

Preheat oven to 450 degrees. Split bagels in half and place on baking sheet, cut side up. Top each half with pizza sauce and other ingredients as desired, ending with cheese. Bake for 10 to 12 minutes or until cheese melts and begins to bubble.

HUSH PUPPIES

Oil

2 cups yellow cornmeal

2 tablespoons flour

1 tablespoon sugar

2 teaspoons salt

Pepper to taste

Hot water

¼ cup milk

¼ cup finely chopped onion

1 egg

2 teaspoons baking powder

Heat oil in deep skillet or fryer to 375 degrees. Mix all dry ingredients except baking powder. Pour in enough hot water to make thick mush, making sure all ingredients are moist. Add milk, onion, egg, and baking powder and mix thoroughly. Use small ice cream scoop to drop spoonfuls of mixture into hot oil, and fry until golden brown.

CREAM OF BROCCOLI SOUP

1 (10 ounce) package frozen chopped broccoli

Onion or onion powder to taste

1 can chicken broth

1 can condensed cream of celery soup

1 can condensed cream of mushroom soup

1 to 1½ cups shredded cheddar cheese

Cook broccoli and onion in chicken broth. Combine soups and stir into broccoli mixture. Bring to a gentle boil, stirring constantly. Add cheese, stirring until melted. Serve hot.

BLACK BEAN SOUP

1 (15 ounce) can black beans, drained

1 (10 ounce) can beef broth

1 soup can water

1 cup tomato juice

¼ teaspoon rosemary

¼ teaspoon sweet basil

1 teaspoon lemon juice

Combine all ingredients except lemon juice and simmer for 20 minutes. Add lemon juice after removing from heat.

CHILI

2 pounds lean ground beef, browned

5 tablespoons chili powder (more or less to taste)

2 cups water

1 onion, finely chopped

2 (15 ounce) cans diced tomatoes

1 (15 ounce) can red beans

1 (15 ounce) can pinto beans

Combine all ingredients and simmer for 20 to 30 minutes.

. . . .

POTATO SOUP

5 large potatoes

2 (10 ounce) cans cheddar cheese soup

1 cup sour cream

2½ cups milk

Salt and pepper to taste

Peel potatoes and cut into cubes. Boil potatoes for 15 to 20 minutes or until soft. Drain. Add soup and sour cream. Gently mix until blended. Add milk, salt, and pepper. Stir well. Heat on medium heat until soup is warm.

 GIVE THANKS

At dinner tonight, start a new notebook and have each family member tell something he or she is thankful for today. Allow a different person to record all the answers each time. Keep this handy to use daily or weekly for recording thankfulness, prayer requests, and future dinner ideas.

• • • • •

Rejoice always, pray continually, give thanks in all circumstances; for this is God's will for you in Christ Jesus.
1 THESSALONIANS 5:16–18 NIV

FESTIVE CHEF'S SALAD

1 head romaine lettuce

2 cooked chicken breasts, cut into strips

1 tomato, sliced

2 hard-boiled eggs, sliced

12 whole black olives

1 ripe avocado, cubed

1 red bell pepper, chopped

Dressing:

2 tablespoons apple cider vinegar

1 tablespoon ketchup

4 tablespoons olive oil

¼ teaspoon salt

¼ teaspoon freshly ground black pepper

Mix all dressing ingredients and chill. Tear lettuce into 2-inch pieces and place in mixing bowl. Add remaining ingredients. Pour dressing over salad. Toss gently.

SHRIMP-BACON BITES

1 cup cleaned cooked shrimp
   (or 1 can)
½ clove garlic, slivered

½ cup chili sauce
8 to 10 slices bacon

Mix shrimp and garlic; pour chili sauce over mixture. Cover and refrigerate for several hours, stirring occasionally. Cut bacon slices in half. Fry until partially cooked; drain. Wrap each shrimp in bacon piece; secure with toothpick. Broil 2 to 3 inches from heat until bacon is crisp.

GUACAMOLE BITES

2 tubes refrigerated
  crescent rolls
½ teaspoon cumin
½ teaspoon chili powder
1 (8 ounce) package cream
  cheese, softened
1 container (1½ cups)
  guacamole or 3 ripe
  avocados, mashed
1 tomato, chopped
¼ cup bacon bits
¼ cup sliced ripe olives

Unroll crescent rolls; place on ungreased baking sheet. Press to seal perforations. Sprinkle with cumin and chili powder; bake at 375 degrees for 17 minutes or until golden brown. Cool. Blend cream cheese and guacamole until smooth; spread over crust. Chill. Top with remaining ingredients and cut into squares.

PIZZA WRAPS

4 to 6 slices turkey
  pepperoni
1 slice provolone cheese
1 flour tortilla

Place pepperoni and cheese on tortilla and roll up. Dip in warm pizza sauce if desired.

EASY ROLL-UPS

1 (8 ounce) package cream cheese, softened

1 cup light sour cream

1 cup finely shredded cheddar cheese

1 (4 ounce) can chopped black olives

2 tablespoons ranch dressing

1 teaspoon salt

10 flour tortillas

Mix all ingredients except tortillas thoroughly. Spread ⅛ cup of mixture on each tortilla. Roll tightly and wrap in plastic wrap. Cover and refrigerate for at least 2 hours. Slice. Serve with salsa if desired.

APPLE CHICKEN SALAD

2 (5 ounce) cans chicken breast, drained

¼ cup mayonnaise

¼ cup chopped sweet onion

1 small apple, chopped

1 teaspoon seasoned salt

Croissants

4 slices swiss cheese

Mix chicken, mayonnaise, onion, apple, and salt together. Slice croissants and place 1 slice of cheese on the side. Top with desired amount of chicken salad.

BACON CHEDDAR DEVILED EGGS

12 hard-boiled eggs, peeled and cut in half

½ cup mayonnaise

4 slices bacon, cooked and crumbled

2 tablespoons finely shredded cheddar cheese

1 tablespoon mustard

Remove yolks from eggs and place in small bowl. Mash egg yolks with remaining ingredients. Fill egg white halves with yolk mixture and refrigerate until serving.

. . . .

PIZZA BREAD STICKS

1 (13.8 ounce) tube refrigerated pizza crust

1 tablespoon butter, melted

1 teaspoon garlic salt

¼ teaspoon oregano

1 (8 ounce) jar prepared pizza sauce

Cut pizza dough into strips. Place on greased cookie sheet and brush with butter. Then sprinkle with garlic salt and oregano. Bake at 350 degrees for 12 to 15 minutes or until golden brown. Serve warm with pizza sauce.

EASY SWEET POTATO FRIES

2 tablespoons frozen orange
  juice concentrate, thawed
1 teaspoon onion powder
½ teaspoon salt
¼ teaspoon pepper
½ teaspoon cinnamon
1 pound sweet potatoes, cut
  into ½-inch sticks

Line cookie sheet with foil and spray with cooking spray.
Combine all ingredients except potatoes. Mix well. Add potato
sticks and mix to coat. Arrange sticks on foil in a single layer.
Bake at 425 degrees for 30 minutes, turning every 10 minutes.

EASY CRACKER DIP

1 (8 ounce) package cream
  cheese, softened
1 small jar cocktail sauce
1 can small shrimp or
  crabmeat

In round dish, layer ingredients in order given. Serve with
crackers.

FRIED CABBAGE

2 tablespoons vegetable oil

3 cups shredded cabbage

1 cup chopped green bell pepper

½ teaspoon salt

Dash pepper

2 cups fresh diced tomatoes

½ cup chopped onion

½ teaspoon sugar

1 cup chopped celery

Heat vegetable oil in frying pan and add all ingredients. Cook for 10 minutes or until vegetables are tender.

GREEN PEAS WITH CELERY AND ONION

2 (10 ounce) packages frozen
  peas

½ cup sliced celery

1 small onion, thinly sliced

3 tablespoons margarine or
  butter, softened

¼ teaspoon salt

Following directions on package for peas, cook celery, onion, and peas; drain. Stir in margarine and salt.

. . . .

TANGY RANCH GREEN BEANS

2 tablespoons butter or
  margarine

2 packages frozen French-
  cut green beans, partially
  thawed

1 can sliced mushrooms,
  drained

1 package dry ranch dressing
  mix

3 to 4 slices bacon, cooked and
  crumbled

In large skillet, melt butter. Stir in green beans and cook until tender. Mix in mushrooms and ranch dressing mix. Heat through. Before serving, sprinkle crumbled bacon over beans.

CHICKEN BITES

4 boneless, skinless chicken breasts

1 cup finely crushed butter-flavored crackers (about 24)

½ cup grated Parmesan cheese

¼ cup finely chopped walnuts

1 teaspoon dried thyme

1 teaspoon dried basil

½ teaspoon seasoned salt

¼ teaspoon pepper

½ cup margarine or butter, melted

Line 2 baking sheets with foil. Cut chicken into 1-inch pieces. Combine crushed crackers, Parmesan cheese, walnuts, thyme, basil, seasoned salt, and pepper. Preheat oven to 400 degrees. Dip chicken pieces into melted margarine, then into crumb mixture. Place on baking sheets and bake uncovered for 20 to 25 minutes or until golden brown.

PARTY POTATOES

10 to 12 medium potatoes, cooked and mashed

1 (8 ounce) package cream cheese, softened

1 cup sour cream

2 tablespoons chopped chives

1 cup shredded cheddar cheese

Salt and pepper to taste

2 tablespoons butter

Beat together all ingredients except butter. Place in greased 9x13-inch baking dish. Cover and refrigerate until 1 hour before serving time. Preheat oven to 350 degrees. Dot potatoes with butter. Bake for 1 hour or until potatoes reach desired tenderness.

CRANBERRY SALAD

1 bag cranberries

1 cup sugar

1 bag mini marshmallows

1 cup chopped nuts

1 (8 ounce) container whipped topping

Crush cranberries in blender. In bowl, combine crushed cranberries and sugar; mix well. Marinate in refrigerator for 2 hours. Fold in marshmallows, nuts, and whipped topping. Refrigerate.

. . . .

STRAWBERRY CHICKEN SALAD

1 (13 ounce) can chunk chicken breast, drained

1 heaping tablespoon mayonnaise

1 pint fresh strawberries

½ cup shaved almonds

In bowl, mix chicken with mayonnaise. Wash strawberries and slice into bite-size pieces over bowl with chicken in it so that all juice from strawberries drips into salad. Drop in strawberries. Pour in almonds. Stir and serve with crackers.

BAKED WATER CHESTNUTS

1 can whole water chestnuts

½ cup soy sauce

Sugar

4 slices bacon, cut in half lengthwise and widthwise

Drain water chestnuts. Marinate in soy sauce for 30 minutes. Drain sauce from water chestnuts and roll each water chestnut in sugar. Wrap in strip of bacon; secure with toothpick. Bake at 400 degrees for 30 minutes.

. . . .

ROMAN PASTA SALAD

1 pound thin spaghetti (or other shaped pasta)

2 large tomatoes

1 large onion

1 large cucumber

1 large green pepper

16 ounces Italian dressing

1 package dry Italian dressing mix

Cook and cool pasta; set aside. Dice vegetables and toss with Italian dressing and dry Italian dressing mix. Add to cool pasta; refrigerate overnight.

TUNA CHEESE SPREAD

1 (8 ounce) package cream
cheese, softened

1 (6 ounce) can tuna, drained
and flaked

½ cup finely chopped green
onion

¼ cup mayonnaise

1 tablespoon lemon juice

¾ teaspoon curry powder

Dash salt

Combine all ingredients. Spread onto bread slices for quick,
tasty sandwiches.

. . . .

CUCUMBERS WITH VINEGAR DRESSING

¼ cup water

¼ cup sugar

¼ cup vinegar

¼ teaspoon salt

Dash pepper

½ small onion, thinly sliced

4 cups cucumbers, peeled and
thinly sliced

Blend water, sugar, vinegar, salt, and pepper; add onion and
cucumbers. Cover and refrigerate for at least 2 hours.

CRAB-STUFFED MUSHROOMS

1 (6 ounce) can crabmeat

1 egg, well beaten

¼ cup dry bread crumbs

¼ cup tomato juice

1 teaspoon lemon juice

Dash Tabasco

2 teaspoons finely chopped celery

1 teaspoon finely chopped onion

½ teaspoon salt

1 pound mushrooms

½ cup dry bread crumbs

¼ cup butter or margarine, melted

Mix first nine ingredients and fill mushroom caps. Toss remaining ½ cup bread crumbs with melted butter and sprinkle over filled caps. Broil 6 inches from heat for 5 to 8 minutes, or bake at 350 degrees for 15 to 20 minutes.

TORTILLA ROLLS

2 (8 ounce) packages cream cheese, softened

1 cup sour cream

1 bunch green onions, diced

1 small jar jalapeño peppers, diced (or black olives)

1 package flour tortillas

1 jar picante sauce

In medium bowl, blend cream cheese, sour cream, green onions, and jalapeño peppers until smooth. Spread thin layer of mixture onto each tortilla and roll up. Place tortillas in pan; cover and refrigerate overnight. Slice each roll into pinwheels. Serve with picante sauce for dipping.

· ·

SHRIMP SPREAD

2 (8 ounce) packages cream cheese, softened

½ cup mayonnaise

½ cup lemon juice

2 (4½ ounce) cans cocktail shrimp, drained, rinsed, and chopped

1 tablespoon prepared horseradish

1 to 2 tablespoons finely chopped green onion

⅛ teaspoon garlic salt

In medium bowl, beat cream cheese until fluffy. Beat in mayonnaise and lemon juice. Stir in shrimp; then add remaining ingredients. Refrigerate to allow flavors to blend. Serve with crackers or vegetables.

Make kitchen cleanup an enjoyable family activity!

 Crank up the music and offer rewards for the best karaoke performance while clearing the table or loading the dishwasher.

 Keep a timer handy and try to beat each family member's time at mopping the floor.

 Give every family member a job and their reward is dessert.

BACON DIP

16 ounces sour cream

½ teaspoon onion powder

1 (16 ounce) package ready-to-serve bacon

½ cup shredded cheddar cheese

1 cup shredded lettuce

1 cup chopped tomatoes

Blend sour cream and onion powder; spread in 9-inch pie pan. Heat bacon as directed on package and cut into small pieces. Sprinkle over sour cream mixture. Top with cheese, lettuce, and tomatoes. Serve with crackers.

. . . .

WILTED LETTUCE SALAD

2 slices bacon, cooked and crumbled

1 tablespoon bacon drippings

2 tablespoons water

2 tablespoons vinegar

Dash salt

2 to 3 tablespoons sugar

1 tablespoon cornstarch

Lettuce

After cooking bacon, remove from heat and pour off all but 1 tablespoon drippings. Add water, vinegar, and salt to slightly cooled drippings; return to heat. Combine sugar and cornstarch; stir into pan mixture and cook until thickened. Add crumbled bacon. Serve hot over lettuce.

DESSERTS AND DRINKS

Gracious words are a honeycomb, sweet to the soul and healing to the bones.

PROVERBS 16:24 NIV

STRAWBERRY TRIFLE

1 angel food cake, cubed

1 small box vanilla instant
    pudding mix

1 cup cold milk

1 pint vanilla ice cream,
    slightly thawed

1 small box strawberry gelatin

1 cup boiling water

1 (10 ounce) package frozen
    strawberries, slightly
    thawed

In 9x9-inch glass baking dish, place cubed angel food cake. In separate bowl, combine pudding mix, milk, and ice cream; beat until smooth and pour over cake. Dissolve gelatin in boiling water. Add strawberries and cool slightly; spoon over pudding layer. Cover and refrigerate overnight.

- -

AMISH PEANUT BUTTER SPREAD

1 quart maple-flavored
    pancake syrup

2 cups creamy peanut butter

1 cup marshmallow crème

Blend all ingredients well. Store in airtight jar. Ready to use immediately on bread or toast.

A tea party is fun for any age and stage of life!

 Create invitations for each member of your family. Tell them to wear their very best clothing.

 Get out the special china (or find a few cups and saucers and a teapot at a thrift store if you don't own any!) and purchase a few flavors of tea. A few English favorites are Earl Grey and English Breakfast Tea.

 Set the table with a white tablecloth and a few fresh-cut flowers.

 Prepare finger foods and tiny sandwiches to place on small china plates (see page 170 for recipes).

 Purchase or prepare a variety of scones with lemon curd and/or Devonshire cream.

 Play a CD or MP3 of piano music to complement your tea party.

 Use the tea party as an avenue to teach manners and proper etiquette to your children.

 With girls: discuss how to act like a lady and dress modestly.

 With boys: discuss how to treat a lady and use proper manners.

A Teatime Prayer:
Heavenly Father, as we enjoy this teatime as a family, allow us to learn from You about kindness and treating each other with love and respect. We are so blessed as a family. We give You all the praise and glory. In Jesus' name, amen.

TEA PARTY QUOTES

You can never get a cup of tea large enough
or a book long enough to suit me.

C. S. LEWIS

• • • • •

My dear, if you could give me a cup of
tea to clear my muddle of a head I should
better understand your affairs.

CHARLES DICKENS

• • • • •

Come and share a pot of tea,
My home is warm and my friendship's free.

EMILIE BARNES

ICED TEA

4 cups water

3 family-sized tea bags or 6 regular-sized tea bags

¾ cup sugar

In medium saucepan, bring water to a boil over high heat. Add tea bags and remove from heat; cover for 10 minutes. Remove tea bags. Add sugar to 1-gallon pitcher. Pour hot tea into pitcher. Fill pitcher with cold water and stir. Cover with lid and store in refrigerator.

QUICK TEA FLAVORINGS

For tea flavoring, dissolve old-fashioned lemon drops or hard mint candy in your tea. They melt fast and keep the tea brisk.

HOT SPICED TEA

½ cup brown sugar

7 cups water, divided

1 teaspoon pumpkin pie spice

2 cans cranberry sauce

¼ cup lemon juice

1 (12 ounce) can frozen orange juice concentrate

Mix brown sugar, 1 cup water, and spice in saucepan. Heat to boiling over high heat, stirring constantly, until sugar is dissolved. Remove from heat. Stir in cranberry sauce and mix well. Stir in remaining water, lemon juice, and orange juice concentrate. Return saucepan to stove and heat mixture to boiling. Reduce heat and let simmer uncovered for 5 minutes.

QUICK 'N' EASY CHERRY COBBLER

2 (20 ounce) cans cherry pie filling

1 box yellow cake mix

1¼ sticks margarine, melted

1 cup chopped walnuts

Pour both cans of pie filling into 9x13-inch baking dish. Spread dry cake mix over filling. Top with melted margarine and walnuts. Bake at 350 degrees for 35 to 45 minutes. Serve warm with vanilla ice cream.

LEMONADE PIE

1 (14 ounce) can sweetened condensed milk

1 (6 ounce) can frozen lemonade concentrate, thawed

1 (8 ounce) container whipped topping, thawed

1 prepared graham cracker piecrust

Beat together condensed milk and lemonade concentrate. Gently fold in whipped topping. Pour into piecrust. Freeze 4 hours or until firm.

PEANUT BUTTER LOGS

1¾ cups powdered sugar

¼ cup butter

1 cup crunchy peanut butter

2 cups crisp rice cereal

Combine powdered sugar and butter in large bowl and beat until smooth. Stir in peanut butter and cereal. Shape dough into finger-sized logs. Place logs on cookie sheet lined with waxed paper. Refrigerate 1 hour. If desired, spread with prepared chocolate frosting. Keep refrigerated.

ORANGE DROPS

1¼ cups vanilla wafers,
   crushed

½ cup flaked coconut

¾ cup powdered sugar

3 ounces frozen orange juice
   concentrate, thawed

Additional powdered sugar

Mix together vanilla wafers, coconut, ¾ cup powdered sugar, and orange juice concentrate. Shape into 1-inch balls and roll in powdered sugar. Store covered in refrigerator.

• • • • •

Sunshine is sweet;
it is good to see the light of day.
People ought to enjoy every day of their lives,
no matter how long they live.

ECCLESIASTES 11:7–8 NCV

CRUNCHY CHOCOLATE COOKIES

1 cup chow mein noodles

2 cups mini marshmallows

2 cups quick oats

1 (12 ounce) bag chocolate chips

1 (12 ounce) bag peanut butter chips

Combine noodles, marshmallows, and oats in large bowl. Stir. In separate bowl, microwave chocolate and peanut butter chips in 30-second intervals until melted. Pour over noodle mixture and stir to coat. Spoon clumps onto waxed paper and cool.

- -

QUICK 'N' EASY CEREAL BARS

½ cup margarine

1 bag large marshmallows

½ cup creamy peanut butter

½ cup raisins

4 cups toasted oats cereal

Melt margarine over low heat in deep saucepan. Stir in marshmallows until smooth and creamy. Mix in peanut butter. Remove from heat; add raisins and cereal, stirring until evenly coated. With buttered hands, press mixture into 9x13-inch pan. Cool; cut into bars.

 ## FOR LITTLE HANDS

The desserts and drinks on the following pages (pages 184–186) are very simple to encourage younger children to learn in the kitchen. Have the child wash his or her hands and help you measure out all the ingredients. Then allow the child to surprise someone else in the family with a special treat!

ROOT BEER FLOAT

1 cup root beer
1 scoop vanilla ice cream

Place root beer in large glass and add ice cream. Try this with other flavors of soda and ice cream such as cola and chocolate ice cream or orange soda and pineapple sherbet.

WORMS IN DIRT

Clear plastic cups
Prepared chocolate pudding

6 chocolate sandwich cookies, crushed
Gummy worms

Layer pudding and crushed cookies in clear plastic cups. Hide worms throughout layers and place 1 to 2 on top.

· ·

STRAWBERRY YOGURT PIE

8 ounces whipped topping
16 ounces strawberry yogurt

1 prepared graham cracker piecrust

Fold whipped topping into yogurt in large bowl. Pour into piecrust. Let chill for at least 3 hours before serving.

· ·

CINNAMON TOAST

1 tablespoon cinnamon
¼ cup sugar

4 slices bread
Butter

Mix together cinnamon and sugar. Toast bread and spread with butter. Sprinkle cinnamon-sugar mixture evenly over top.

EASY MICROWAVE FUDGE

3 cups semisweet chocolate
   chips

1 (14 ounce) can sweetened
   condensed milk

1 teaspoon vanilla

In large microwavable bowl, combine chocolate chips and
sweetened condensed milk. Microwave on high for 2 minutes.
Add vanilla. Stir. Line 8x8-inch pan with waxed paper and pour
in fudge. Refrigerate.

EXTRA-SPECIAL CHOCOLATE MILK

1 cup milk

2 tablespoons chocolate syrup

Whipped cream

Candy-coated chocolate
   pieces or sprinkles

Pour milk into mug. Add syrup and top with desired amount of
whipped cream. Garnish with candy or sprinkles.

BANANA S'MORE SNACKS

Graham cracker squares

Milk chocolate candy bars

Sliced bananas

Large marshmallows

For each snack, top a graham cracker square with a piece of
chocolate, 4 banana slices, and a marshmallow. Microwave for
10 to 12 seconds or until marshmallow is puffed. Place another
graham cracker on top and enjoy.

COCONUT CUSTARD WITH CRUST

5 eggs

½ cup sugar

2 cups milk

½ cup flour

1 cup flaked coconut

2 tablespoons butter

2 teaspoons vanilla

Preheat oven to 350 degrees. In large bowl, mix all ingredients together. Pour into greased deep-dish pie pan. Bake for 45 minutes and allow to cool. Custard should fall a little.

- -

CHOCOLATE PRETZEL RINGS

50 pretzel circles

1 (8 ounce) package
    milk chocolate kisses,
    unwrapped

50 candy-coated chocolate
    pieces (about ½ cup)

Line cookie sheet with waxed paper. Spread pretzels out on sheet. Place chocolate kiss in center of each pretzel. Bake at 275 degrees for 2 to 3 minutes or until chocolate is softened. Immediately place coated candy on each chocolate kiss and press down slightly so that chocolate spreads to touch pretzel. Refrigerate until chocolate is firm. Store at room temperature.

APPLE CRISP

4 cups chopped apples

1 cup sugar

½ teaspoon cinnamon

3 tablespoons flour

½ cup salt

Topping:

½ cup rolled oats

½ cup flour

½ cup brown sugar

⅓ cup melted butter

Preheat oven to 350 degrees. In bowl, mix together apples, sugar, cinnamon, flour, and salt; transfer to baking dish. Mix together oats, flour, brown sugar, and melted butter and pour over apple mixture. Bake for 40 minutes.

FUDGE DROPS

1 cup semisweet chocolate chips, divided

3 tablespoons canola oil

1 cup packed brown sugar

3 egg whites

2 tablespoons plus 1½ teaspoons light corn syrup

1 tablespoon water

2½ teaspoons vanilla

1¾ cups flour

⅔ cup plus 1 tablespoon powdered sugar, divided

⅓ cup baking cocoa

2¼ teaspoons baking powder

⅛ teaspoon salt

Preheat oven to 350 degrees. In bowl, combine ¾ cup chocolate chips with oil and melt in microwave; stir until smooth. Pour into large bowl; cool for 5 minutes. Stir in brown sugar. Add egg whites, corn syrup, water, and vanilla; stir until smooth. In separate bowl, combine flour, ⅔ cup powdered sugar, cocoa, baking powder, and salt; gradually add to chocolate mixture until combined. Stir in remaining ¼ cup chocolate chips (dough will be very stiff). Drop by tablespoonfuls 2 inches apart onto greased baking sheets. Bake for 10 minutes or until puffed and set. Cool for 2 minutes before removing to wire racks. Sprinkle cooled cookies with remaining powdered sugar.

MISSISSIPPI MUD CAKE

3 tablespoons cocoa

2 cups sugar

1 cup butter

1 teaspoon vanilla

4 eggs

1½ cups flour

1⅓ cups flaked coconut

½ cup chopped pecans

1 large jar marshmallow crème

Frosting:

½ cup cocoa

½ cup evaporated milk

1 teaspoon vanilla

1 pound powdered sugar

½ cup butter

½ cup chopped pecans

Preheat oven to 350 degrees. In large bowl, cream cocoa, sugar, and butter. Add vanilla and eggs and mix well. Add flour, coconut, and ½ cup pecans. Beat for 2 minutes. Bake in greased 9x13-inch baking dish for 35 to 40 minutes. While cake is still hot, gently spread marshmallow crème over top and let cool. Frosting: In bowl, beat together cocoa, evaporated milk, vanilla, powdered sugar, and butter until smooth and spread over marshmallow crème. Sprinkle chopped pecans over top.

SUPER-QUICK POUND CAKE

1 box vanilla pudding pound
   cake mix

1 cup flour

1 cup sour cream

1 cup sweet milk

4 eggs

¾ cup sugar

½ teaspoon vanilla

½ teaspoon butter

½ teaspoon almond extract

½ teaspoon lemon extract

Preheat oven to 350 degrees. Combine all ingredients in large mixing bowl and beat for 2 minutes. Pour into greased pound cake baking pan. Bake for 1 hour and 10 minutes. Cool for 5 minutes in pan.

CRUNCHY NOODLE DROPS

3 cups butterscotch chips (or
   semisweet chocolate chips)

1¼ cups chow mein noodles

1 cup peanuts

In medium saucepan, melt butterscotch chips over low heat, stirring constantly until melted. Remove from heat. Stir in noodles and peanuts until well coated. Drop by tablespoons onto waxed paper and cool until firm.

CONFETTI COOKIES

1 cup butter

1 cup packed brown sugar

1 cup sugar

2 eggs

2 teaspoons vanilla

2¼ cups flour

1 teaspoon baking soda

1 cup multicolored candy-coated chocolate pieces

Preheat oven to 375 degrees. In large bowl, stir all ingredients together and drop onto ungreased baking sheet. Bake for 10 minutes. Let cool.

GRANDMA SPENCER'S GRAHAM CRACKER PUDDING

2 (3 ounce) boxes vanilla instant pudding mix

1 box graham crackers

2 (21 ounce) cans cherry pie filling

Mix pudding according to package directions and let set for 5 minutes. Layer graham crackers in bottom of 9x13-inch baking pan. Layer half of pudding on top of graham cracker layer. Pour 1 can cherry pie filling onto vanilla pudding. Repeat layers: another layer of graham crackers, remaining vanilla pudding, remaining cherry pie filling. Refrigerate for several hours before serving.

ICE WATER CHOCOLATE CAKE

¾ cup margarine

2¼ cups sugar

1½ teaspoons vanilla

3 eggs

3 squares baking chocolate, melted

3 cups flour

1½ teaspoons baking soda

¾ teaspoon salt

1½ cups ice water

Blend margarine, sugar, and vanilla until mixture is consistency of whipping cream. Add eggs, one at a time, then chocolate. Sift flour, baking soda, and salt; add to creamy mixture alternately with ice water. Spread in greased 9x13-inch pan and bake at 350 degrees for 45 minutes.

CARAMEL CORN

1½ cups unpopped popcorn

1 cup corn syrup

1 cup brown sugar

2 cups sugar

½ cup butter

3 teaspoons vinegar

1 teaspoon salt

1 teaspoon baking soda

Pop corn and set aside. In large saucepan, combine all but popcorn and baking soda; cook to hard-crack stage. Test readiness in cup of ice water (should separate into hard but flexible threads). Remove from heat and stir in baking soda. Pour over popped corn; stir well to coat.

CHOCOLATE ZUCCHINI CAKE

1 cup brown sugar

½ cup sugar

½ cup margarine

½ cup vegetable oil

3 eggs

1 teaspoon vanilla

½ cup buttermilk

2½ cups flour

½ teaspoon allspice

½ teaspoon cinnamon

½ teaspoon salt

2 teaspoons baking soda

¼ cup cocoa

1¾ cups shredded zucchini, drained

1 cup semisweet chocolate chips

Cream brown sugar, sugar, margarine, and vegetable oil. Add eggs, vanilla, buttermilk, and flour; stir well. Sift allspice, cinnamon, salt, baking soda, and cocoa. Add to creamed mixture and beat well. Stir in zucchini and pour into 9x13-inch pan. Sprinkle chocolate chips on top. Bake at 325 degrees for 45 minutes.

SEVEN-LAYER BARS

½ cup butter or margarine

1 cup crushed graham crackers

1 cup semisweet chocolate chips

1 cup butterscotch chips

½ to 1 cup chopped nuts

1 cup flaked coconut

1 (14 ounce) can sweetened condensed milk

In 9x13-inch pan, cut butter and melt in 350 degree oven to coat bottom. Sprinkle crushed graham crackers on top. Pat down. Sprinkle chocolate and butterscotch chips, nuts, and coconut on top. Drizzle milk evenly over all. Bake for 30 minutes or until lightly browned.

CHOCOLATE-COVERED CRACKERS

1½ cups semisweet chocolate chips

1 tablespoon shortening

3 dozen peanut butter sandwich crackers

Combine chocolate chips and shortening in 1-quart saucepan and cook over low heat until melted. Remove from heat; using fork, dip crackers into mixture until coated. Place on cookie sheet lined with waxed paper and refrigerate until chocolate hardens. If chocolate starts to harden while dipping, return saucepan to low heat.

SNOWY CINNAMON COCOA

4 cups milk

1 cup chocolate syrup

1 teaspoon cinnamon

Frozen whipped topping, thawed

¼ cup semisweet chocolate chips

Place milk and chocolate syrup in microwave-safe bowl and stir. Cook on high for 3 to 4 minutes or until hot. Stir in cinnamon. Pour into 4 large mugs and garnish with whipped topping and chocolate chips.

MEXICAN COFFEE

¾ cup ground dark-roast coffee

3 teaspoons ground cinnamon

6 cups water

1 cup milk

⅓ cup chocolate syrup

2 tablespoons light brown sugar

1 teaspoon vanilla

Whipped topping

Place coffee and cinnamon in filter basket of coffeemaker. Pour water in machine and brew coffee. In saucepan, blend milk, chocolate syrup, and brown sugar. Stir over low heat until sugar dissolves. Combine milk mixture with brewed coffee in pot and stir in vanilla. Garnish servings with whipped topping and sprinkle with additional cinnamon.

THE ULTIMATE CHOCOLATE CHIP BAR

1 cup butter, melted

1 cup brown sugar

1 cup sugar

2 eggs

1 teaspoon vanilla

2 cups flour

½ teaspoon salt

1 teaspoon baking soda

½ teaspoon baking powder

2 cups quick oats

24 ounces semisweet chocolate chips

In large bowl, mix ingredients in order given; spread in greased 9x13-inch pan. Bake at 350 degrees for 20 to 25 minutes. Cool and cut into squares.

PUPPY CHOW

12 ounces semisweet chocolate chips

½ cup butter

1 cup peanut butter

1 box crisp corn cereal squares

1 pound powdered sugar, divided

Melt chocolate chips, butter, and peanut butter. Stir in cereal and coat well. Put half of mixture in large plastic ziplock bag with half of powdered sugar; shake well. Repeat with second half. Store in airtight container.

WASSAIL

2 quarts apple cider

2 (14 ounce) cans pineapple juice

2 cups orange juice

1 cup lemon juice

1 stick whole cinnamon

1 teaspoon whole cloves

1 cup sugar

Combine all ingredients in large pot and simmer for 5 minutes. Strain and refrigerate overnight. Reheat and serve warm.

. . . .

HOT CHOCOLATE

1 (1 pound) can powdered chocolate drink mix

1 pound sugar

1 (8 quart) box powdered sugar

1 (3 to 6 ounce) jar powdered creamer

Sift all ingredients together. Store in airtight container. For one mug of hot chocolate, add 4 heaping teaspoons of mixture to 1 cup boiling water.

CAKE IN A MUG

4 tablespoons flour

4 tablespoons sugar

2 tablespoons cocoa

1 egg

3 tablespoons milk

3 tablespoons oil

3 tablespoons mini chocolate chips

⅛ teaspoon vanilla

Whipped cream

Add dry ingredients to large microwavable mug and mix well. Add egg and mix thoroughly. Add milk and oil. Mix well. Add chocolate chips and vanilla, and mix again. Microwave on high for 3 minutes. Cake will rise over top of mug. Allow to cool a little, top with whipped cream, and serve.

OHIO BUCKEYES

8 ounces creamy peanut butter

1 stick butter

1¾ cups powdered sugar

1 (12 ounce) package milk chocolate chips

Mix peanut butter and butter until creamy. Add sugar gradually. Refrigerate for 30 minutes. Roll peanut butter mixture into 1-inch balls. Set on cookie sheets covered with waxed paper and freeze until firm. Melt chocolate in microwave on high for 2 minutes. Do not overheat. Stir. Insert toothpick into frozen peanut butter ball and dip into chocolate to cover almost the entire ball. Let cool on waxed paper. Keep refrigerated.

CHERRIES IN THE SNOW

½ cup butter

½ cup brown sugar

2 cups flour

1 cup chopped pecans

1 (8 ounce) package cream cheese

2 tablespoons vanilla

1 cup powdered sugar

1 (8 ounce) container whipped topping

1 (15 ounce) can cherry pie filling

Preheat oven to 350 degrees. Melt butter and mix in bowl with brown sugar, flour, and pecans. Pat mixture lightly into 9x13-inch baking pan. Bake for 20 minutes and let cool for 5 minutes. In bowl, combine cream cheese, vanilla, powdered sugar, and whipped topping. Spread over warm crust. Top with cherry pie filling and refrigerate. Serve chilled.

BISCUIT COFFEE CAKE

2 tubes refrigerated buttermilk biscuits

⅓ cup firmly packed brown sugar

¼ cup butter, melted

1 teaspoon cinnamon

⅓ cup pecans

Preheat oven to 350 degrees. In lightly greased 9x9-inch pan, arrange biscuits, overlapping edges. Combine remaining ingredients and spread evenly over biscuits. Bake for 15 minutes or until done.

PIÑA COLADA CAKE

1 box yellow cake mix

1 small can crushed pineapple

1 (14 ounce) can sweetened
  condensed milk

1 small can cream of coconut

Whipped topping

Flaked coconut

Make yellow cake using 9x13-inch pan according to directions on box. While still hot, poke holes in cake and pour pineapple, sweetened condensed milk, and cream of coconut over it. Let cake cool and top with whipped topping. Garnish with flaked coconut.

CHOCOLATE-DRIZZLED KETTLE CORN

2 bags microwave kettle corn

½ cup semisweet or milk
  chocolate chips

Pop bags of microwave kettle corn and spread in large baking pan. Microwave chocolate chips on high for 30 seconds. Stir. Repeat until chips are melted. Dip fork into chocolate and drizzle over kettle corn. Allow to cool before serving.

PEACH FOLDOVERS

1 (10 ounce) tube
    refrigerated biscuits
⅔ cup sugar
¾ teaspoon cinnamon

¼ teaspoon nutmeg
1¼ cups fresh peaches,
    peeled and chopped
¼ cup butter, melted

Preheat oven to 375 degrees. Roll out dough from two biscuits each into 4-inch circles. In small bowl, stir sugar, cinnamon, and nutmeg together. Place 2 tablespoons chopped peaches onto one side of each dough circle. Sprinkle 1 teaspoon sugar mixture over peaches. Fold dough in half. Use fork to seal edges. Dip each foldover in butter and then in remaining sugar mixture. Bake on ungreased cookie sheet for 15 to 20 minutes.

FROZEN FRUIT POPSICLES

Plastic cups
Various fruit juices

Canned peaches, pears, or
    mandarin oranges
Popsicle sticks

Fill plastic cup halfway with your favorite fruit juice. Add chunks of fruit and freeze. Halfway through freezing, place a Popsicle stick in the center. Freeze until solid.

CINNAMON STICKY BUNS

1 cup packed brown sugar

½ cup corn syrup

½ cup butter

1 cup chopped pecans

½ cup sugar

¼ cup cinnamon

2 (16.3 ounce) tubes large
   refrigerated biscuits

Mix brown sugar, corn syrup, and butter in saucepan. Cook until sugar dissolves, stirring constantly. Add pecans. Spoon into greased 9x13-inch pan. In shallow bowl, mix sugar and cinnamon. Cut each biscuit in half and roll in cinnamon-sugar mixture. Bake at 375 degrees for 25 to 30 minutes or until golden brown. Invert onto platter and serve.

FROZEN APPLESAUCE FRUIT SNACK

1 cup applesauce

1 (10 ounce) package frozen
   strawberries, thawed

1 (11 ounce) can mandarin
   oranges, drained

2 tablespoons orange juice

Combine all ingredients in large bowl. Spoon fruit mixture into paper cups. Freeze until firm. Remove from freezer about 30 minutes before serving.

PECAN SUGAR BALLS

½ cup butter

2 tablespoons honey

½ teaspoon vanilla

1 cup flour

2 cups chopped pecans

Red or green sugar sprinkles

Preheat oven to 350 degrees. In small bowl, mix butter and honey with electric mixer. Add vanilla, flour, and pecans; stir well. Shape into 1-inch balls and place on ungreased cookie sheet. Bake for 12 to 14 minutes. Cool slightly and roll in sugar sprinkles.

BUTTERSCOTCH

2 cups sugar

⅔ cup dark corn syrup

¼ cup water

¼ cup heavy cream

In saucepan, combine all ingredients. Stir over low heat until sugar is dissolved. Raise heat to medium and bring to a boil. Boil until candy thermometer reaches 300 degrees. Pour candy into buttered 9x13-inch pan. Let cool. Score into 1-inch squares. When cooled completely, break into pieces.

ICEBOX DESSERT

¾ cup butter

1 cup chopped pecans

1½ cups flour

1 cup powdered sugar

1 (8 ounce) package cream
    cheese, softened

1 (8 ounce) container whipped
    topping, divided

1 (3 ounce) box vanilla instant
    pudding mix

1 (3 ounce) box your favorite
    flavor instant pudding mix

3 cups milk

Preheat oven to 350 degrees. Melt butter, and combine in bowl with pecans and flour. Press into greased 9x13-inch baking pan. Bake for 10 minutes or until lightly browned. Cool. In bowl, cream together powdered sugar and cream cheese. Fold in 1 cup whipped topping; spoon over cooled crust. In another bowl, combine both boxes of instant pudding mix and milk. Mix well and pour over cream cheese mixture. Top with remaining whipped topping. Refrigerate several hours before serving.

CHOCOLATE TRUFFLES

⅔ cup heavy whipping cream   2 teaspoons vanilla

2 cups semisweet or milk
   chocolate chips

In saucepan, heat cream almost to a boil. Remove from heat
and add chocolate chips. Whisk gently until chocolate is
melted and mixture is smooth. Stir in vanilla and pour into
bowl. Cover and refrigerate for 3 hours or until firm. When
chocolate mixture is solid enough to work with, scoop into
1-inch balls and roll in your favorite coatings, such as crushed
cookies, sprinkles, powdered sugar, flaked coconut, chopped
nuts, or colored sugars. Cover and refrigerate for 2 hours. Serve
cold. Keep refrigerated in airtight container.

PUMPKIN PIE SMOOTHIE

1 cup crushed ice   ½ cup vanilla yogurt

½ cup pumpkin puree   1 tablespoon brown sugar

½ cup pineapple chunks   1 whole graham cracker

1½ cups orange juice   ½ teaspoon pumpkin pie spice

Place ice in bottom of blender. Add remaining ingredients.
Puree until smooth. Serve immediately with a sprinkle of
cinnamon.

NUTRITIOUS NO-BAKE COOKIES

½ cup peanut butter

½ cup honey or corn syrup

¼ cup orange juice

1½ cups nonfat dry milk

4 cups crispy cereal mix

Mix first four ingredients thoroughly. Add crispy cereal mix. Shape into small balls.

. . . .

FUDGE BARS

1½ cups semisweet chocolate chips

1½ cups butterscotch chips

1 (7 ounce) can sweetened condensed milk

½ teaspoon vanilla

Melt chocolate chips, butterscotch chips, and milk in saucepan over low heat, stirring until smooth. Remove from heat and stir in vanilla. Pour into 8x8-inch pan and refrigerate until firm. Cut into 1-inch bars.

KRISTY'S NO-BAKE DELIGHTS

2 cups sugar

3 tablespoons cocoa

½ cup margarine

½ cup milk

⅛ teaspoon salt

3 cups quick oats

½ cup peanut butter

1 teaspoon vanilla

In heavy saucepan, bring sugar, cocoa, margarine, milk, and salt to a rapid boil for 1 minute. Add quick oats, peanut butter, and vanilla; mix well. Working quickly, drop by spoonfuls onto waxed paper and let cool.

PEACH SMOOTHIE

1 cup crushed ice

2 cups fresh or frozen peaches, peeled and sliced

½ cup pineapple juice

½ cup milk

¼ cup vanilla yogurt

Place ice in bottom of blender. Add remaining ingredients. Puree until smooth. Serve immediately.

MANDARIN ORANGE PIE

1 cup whipped cream

2 cups orange-flavored yogurt

½ cup canned mandarin orange slices, drained

1 graham cracker piecrust

Fold whipped cream into yogurt in large bowl. Stir in oranges. Pour into piecrust. Cover with plastic wrap. Refrigerate for at least 3 hours before serving. You can also freeze this pie and thaw slightly before serving.

PEANUT BUTTER DROPS

12 ounces peanut butter chips

1 cup peanut butter

4 cups cornflakes cereal

½ cup cocktail peanuts

Melt peanut butter chips and peanut butter over low heat, stirring constantly. Remove from heat and stir in cereal and peanuts until well coated. Drop by tablespoons onto waxed paper and cool until firm.

GRAMMY'S PEANUT BUTTER PIE

¾ cup powdered sugar
⅓ cup peanut butter
1 refrigerated pie shell, baked

1 (8 ounce) box vanilla
    pudding, prepared
2 cups whipped topping

In small bowl, use pastry blender to combine powdered sugar and peanut butter; set aside. Line pie shell with one-third of peanut butter mixture. Spread pudding evenly on top. Top with whipped topping and sprinkle remaining peanut butter mixture evenly over pie. Chill well.

BROWNIE PIZZA

1 (15 ounce) box fudge brownie mix, prepared according to package directions

½ cup peanut butter

½ cup mini chocolate chips

1 (6 ounce) package candy-coated milk chocolate pieces

Grease 12-inch pizza pan. Pour prepared brownie mix onto pizza pan. Bake at 350 degrees for 15 minutes or until done in center. Remove from oven and let cool for 2 minutes. Drop peanut butter and mini chips onto brownie and let sit for 30 seconds or until peanut butter is melted and easily spreadable. Spread over brownie and top with candy pieces.

CHOCOLATE BANANA SMOOTHIE

1 cup crushed ice

2 large bananas

1½ cups milk

¼ cup vanilla yogurt

3 tablespoons chocolate instant breakfast mix

Place ice in bottom of blender. Add remaining ingredients. Puree until smooth. Serve immediately.

CREAM CHEESE BARS

1 box lemon cake mix
½ cup butter
3 eggs, divided

1 (8 ounce) package cream cheese
1 package lemon frosting mix

Preheat oven to 350 degrees. In bowl, combine cake mix, butter, and 1 egg; stir until moist. Press mixture into greased 9x13-inch baking dish. In separate bowl, mix cream cheese and frosting mix until smooth; set aside ½ cup for topping. To remaining cream cheese mixture add 2 eggs and beat for 4 minutes. Spread onto cake mixture and bake for 35 minutes. Let cool and then spread ½ cup reserved frosting mixture (add a little water if mixture has become stiff) over top.

ORANGE BANANA SMOOTHIE

1 cup crushed ice
½ cup frozen orange juice concentrate
1 cup skim milk

1 medium banana
½ cup vanilla yogurt
1 tablespoon honey

Place ice in bottom of blender. Add remaining ingredients. Puree until smooth. Serve immediately.

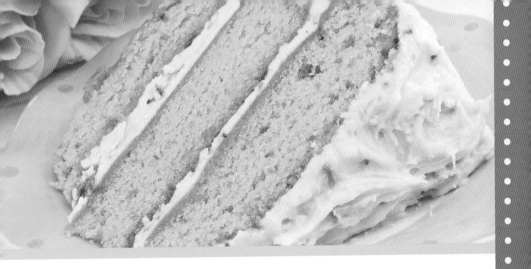

STRAWBERRY JELL-O CAKE

½ cup water

1 (3 ounce) box
    strawberry gelatin

1 box white cake mix

1 cup vegetable oil

4 eggs

3 tablespoons flour

1 cup strawberries (fresh or
    frozen)

Frosting:

½ cup butter, softened

1 pound powdered sugar

⅓ cup strawberries

Preheat oven to 350 degrees. Bring water to a boil. Stir in
gelatin and set aside. In separate bowl, combine cake mix and
oil. Mix until smooth. Add eggs and flour. Mix until smooth
again. Add gelatin and strawberries. Pour into greased 9x13-
inch baking pan. Bake for 35 minutes or until cake tests
done. Frosting: Blend softened butter, powdered sugar, and
strawberries until smooth. Frost cooled cake.

APPLE-CRANBERRY DUMP CAKE

1 (16 ounce) can whole-cranberry sauce

1 (21 ounce) can apple pie filling

1 box yellow cake mix

4 ounces butter

½ cup chopped pecans

Whipped topping

Dump cranberries into ungreased 9x13-inch baking pan. Dump apple pie filling into pan. Spread mixture evenly and spread dry cake mix on top. Cut up butter and dot top of cake. Sprinkle pecans over cake mix and butter. Bake at 325 degrees for 65 minutes or until wooden pick inserted in center comes out clean. Let cool. Top with whipped topping and serve.

BANANA MILKSHAKE SMOOTHIE

1 cup crushed ice

2 large bananas

1 (15 ounce) can pineapple chunks, undrained

1 cup skim milk

1 cup banana yogurt

Place ice in bottom of blender. Add remaining ingredients. Puree until smooth. Serve immediately.

EASY MINI CHEESECAKES

1 dozen vanilla wafers

2 (8 ounce) packages cream cheese

1 teaspoon vanilla

½ cup sugar

2 eggs

Line muffin pan with 12 foil liners. Place a vanilla wafer in each liner. In mixing bowl, combine cream cheese, vanilla, and sugar. Beat well. Add eggs and beat until well blended. Pour cream cheese mixture over wafers. Fill each liner about three-quarters full. Bake at 325 degrees for 25 minutes. Garnish with fruit or chocolate.

BANANA POPS

3 bananas, peeled and halved

6 Popsicle sticks

½ cup peanut butter

¼ cup crispy rice cereal

Push a Popsicle stick through cut end of each banana. Spread peanut butter on bananas and roll in cereal. Wrap in waxed paper and freeze for 3 hours.

STRAWBERRY CREAM CHEESE CRESCENTS

1 (8 ounce) tube refrigerated
    crescent rolls

Cream cheese
Strawberry preserves

Unroll crescent rolls and fill each with 1 tablespoon cream cheese and 1 to 2 teaspoons strawberry preserves. Roll up. Bake according to package directions.

. . . .

CHOCOLATE ICE CREAM BALLS

3 cups chocolate ice cream
1½ cups semisweet chocolate
    chips

15 chocolate sandwich cookies,
    crushed
½ cup milk chocolate chips,
    melted

Mix ice cream and chocolate chips. Using ice cream scoop, scoop ice cream mixture into six balls. Roll in crushed cookies. Place on cookie sheet lined with waxed paper and freeze for 2 hours or until firm. Place frozen ice cream balls on wire rack. Spoon melted chocolate over each ball. Freeze again until firm, at least 1 hour. Remove from freezer 10 minutes before serving.

LEMON BARS

1 (18 ounce) package lemon cake mix with pudding

1 egg

½ cup vegetable oil

1 (8 ounce) package cream cheese

¼ cup sugar

1 tablespoon lemon juice

Combine cake mix, egg, and oil. Mix well. Reserve 1 cup for topping and press rest into ungreased 9x13-inch pan with fork. Bake at 350 degrees for 15 minutes. Cool. In medium bowl, beat cream cheese, sugar, and lemon juice until smooth. Spread evenly over crust. Crumble reserved cake mix over top. Bake for 15 minutes or until filling is set. Cool and serve.

BANANA BARS

¾ cup butter, softened

1 cup brown sugar

1 egg

3 ripe bananas

½ teaspoon ground cinnamon

½ teaspoon salt

4 cups quick oats

½ cup raisins or chocolate chips

In large mixing bowl, cream butter and brown sugar. Add egg, bananas, cinnamon, and salt. Mix well. Add remaining ingredients and mix. Spread into greased 9x13-inch pan. Bake at 350 degrees for 45 to 50 minutes or until toothpick comes out clean. Allow bars to cool before cutting into squares.

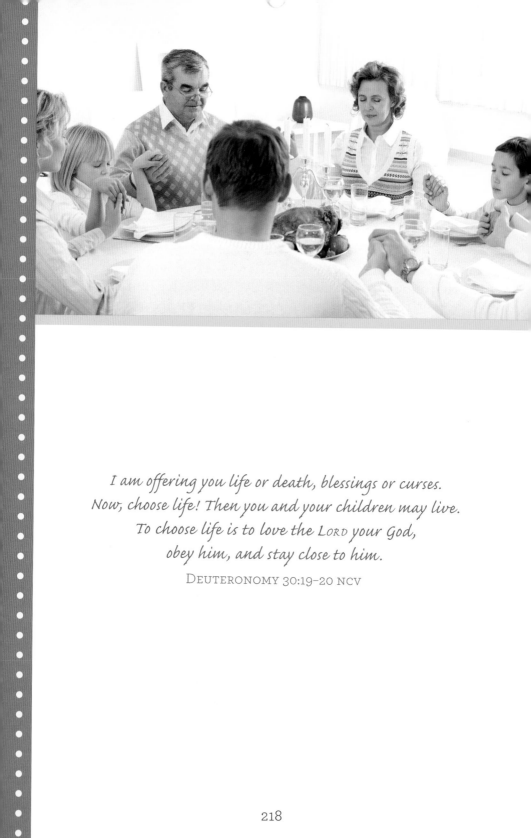

I am offering you life or death, blessings or curses.
Now, choose life! Then you and your children may live.
To choose life is to love the LORD your God,
obey him, and stay close to him.

DEUTERONOMY 30:19–20 NCV

FROZEN PUMPKIN DESSERT

1 (8 ounce) package cream
cheese, softened
½ cup sugar
¼ cup brown sugar
1 (16 ounce) can pumpkin

1 teaspoon pumpkin pie spice
1 (8 ounce) container whipped
topping, thawed, divided
Slivered almonds, chopped
(optional)

Beat cream cheese and sugars until well blended. Add pumpkin
and spice. Mix well. Reserve ½ cup whipped topping. Gently
add remaining whipped topping. Pour into 9x9-inch baking
pan. Freeze for 4 hours or until firm. Top with reserved whipped
topping. Add chopped slivered almonds if desired.

PEANUT BUTTER CUP BROWNIES

1 (18.3 ounce) box brownie mix
Miniature peanut butter cups, unwrapped

Preheat oven to 350 degrees. Prepare brownie mixture as
directed on package. Fill greased mini muffin cups two-thirds
full. Press peanut butter cup into center of each muffin cup. Do
not overflow. Bake for 10 to 15 minutes. Do not overbake.

MONKEY BREAD

1 cup sugar

2 teaspoons cinnamon

3 tubes refrigerated biscuits, cut into quarters

½ cup chopped nuts

½ cup butter

1 cup brown sugar

Combine sugar and cinnamon in large plastic bag. Add biscuits and shake. Place coated biscuits and nuts in greased Bundt pan. Boil butter with brown sugar for 1 minute; pour over biscuits. Bake at 350 degrees for 30 to 35 minutes. Remove from pan immediately. Best when served warm.

FRUIT PIZZA

1 (20 ounce) package refrigerated sugar cookie dough

1 (8 ounce) package cream cheese, softened

⅓ cup sugar

½ teaspoon vanilla

Assorted fresh fruit, sliced

½ cup raspberry preserves

2 tablespoons cold water

Press cookie dough into round or rectangular pizza pan. Bake at 375 degrees for 12 minutes or until golden brown. Cool. Meanwhile, beat cream cheese, sugar, and vanilla until smooth. Spread over crust. Arrange fruit over cream cheese layer. Mix preserves and water and spoon over fruit. Refrigerate. Cut into wedges.

RECIPE INDEX

KID-FRIENDLY FAVORITES

FAVORITE CLASSICS

TRY SOMETHING NEW!

SOUPS, VEGGIES, AND APPETIZERS

DESSERTS AND DRINKS